ANIMATION Rules!

ANIMATION Rules!

52 ways you can achieve creative success

written and illustrated by

STEVE HICKNER

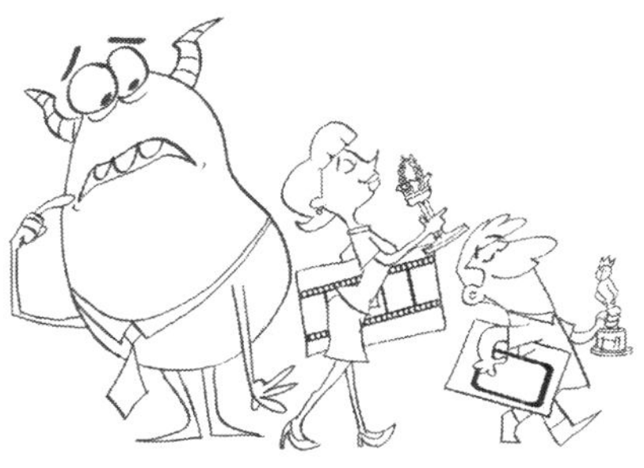

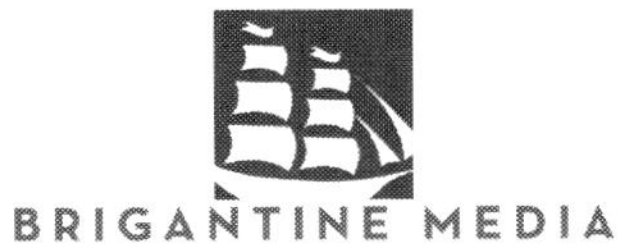

BRIGANTINE MEDIA

Illustrations by Steve Hickner

Brigantine Media
211 North Avenue, St. Johnsbury, Vermont 05819
Phone: 802-751-8802 | Fax: 802-751-8804
Email: neil@brigantinemedia.com
Website: www.brigantinemedia.com

ISBN 978-1-9384063-8-6

Dedication

For Jim, who set me on this journey, and
Kay, who was my Guardian Angel.

Acknowledgments

Each creative endeavor begins with an idea, and the origin for this book belongs to Neil Raphel. Without his tireless dedication, there would be no series of *Rules!* books. Janis Raye is the other proud parent of this book. Her wise edits and great choices helped guide this ugly duckling towards being a swan.

Every thought, every word, every lesson in this book is the result of the experiences that I have gained from my animation colleagues and friends over the past thirty-five years. They are the true authors—I only transcribed their wisdom.

The Rules

PART ONE: DO THE RIGHT THING

PART TWO: PORTFOLIOS, PRESENTATIONS, AND PITCHES

PART THREE: IMPROVE YOURSELF

PART ONE

Do the Right Thing

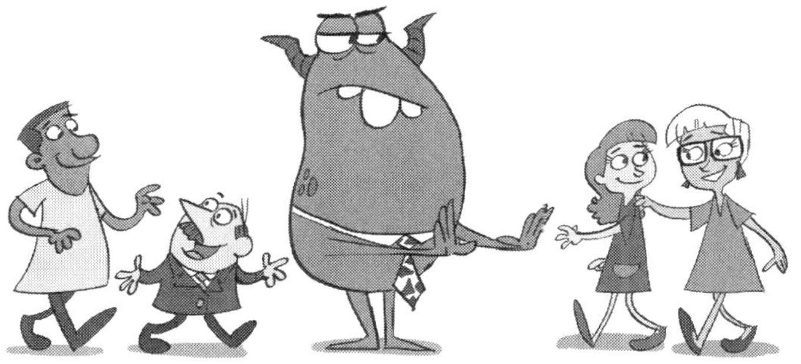

RULE

1

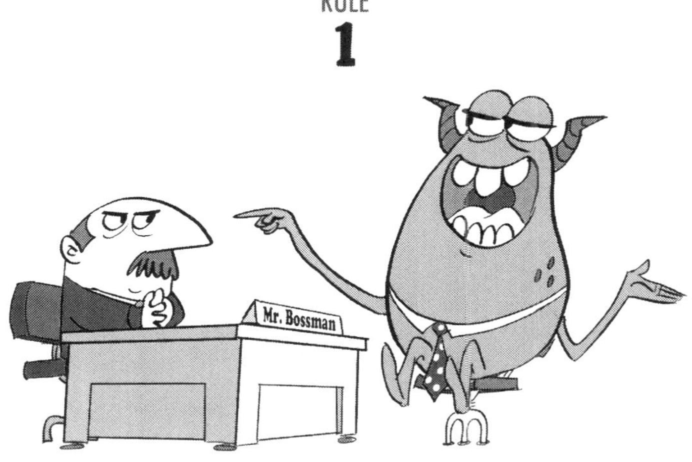

Put in your time before you take someone else's time.

SUPPOSE YOU WERE a major league pitcher. Would you make your opening pitch without studying the opposing batters? If you were the starting quarterback for an NFL team, would you take your first snap from center without studying the other team's defense? Not if you wanted to stay in the major leagues.

Start your job hunt by first researching the employers.

As an artist looking for work, you need to be selling what the buyer is buying. Make sure your sales pitch lines up with the employer's needs by knowing the kind of product the employer makes and the kind of people the employer hires. Learn about the companies you are interested in working for.

On too many occasions, young people call me seeking advice about getting into the animation business, and it is obvious that they haven't done their homework about the industry. I no longer try to educate them. Now, if they haven't studied the animation industry, I quickly end the conversation.

You don't get *my time* until you have put in *your time*.

RULE

2

Soak in where you are.

TWO WEEKS BEFORE commencement, I visited a large university where I met a graduating senior who admitted to me that he didn't have a portfolio or demo reel. I couldn't believe it. How could he study animation for four years and end up with nothing to present?

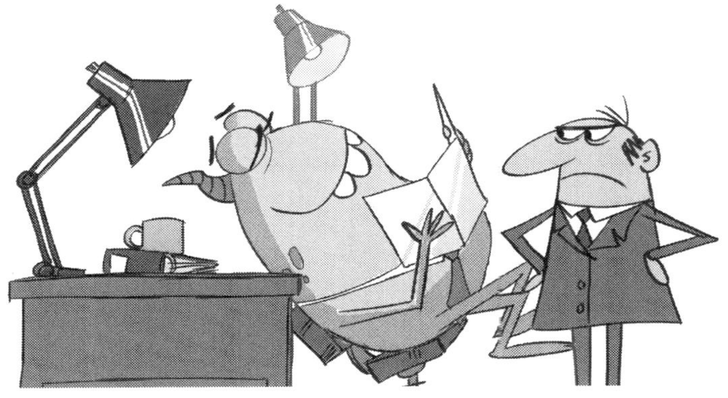

At another college, a student asked if I would mentor him while he made his student film. I agreed to help and encouraged him to send me his work. As it turned out, it was the easiest mentoring job that I have ever had. I never heard from him again.

On a big animated feature, I remember a storyboard artist who was new to the studio, and was working with a group of seasoned professionals. The artist was offered the opportunity to pair with a more experienced artist, but he declined. He also turned down the chance to attend lunchtime story classes and drawing lessons. When he was laid off, he blamed others, not himself.

Life is not a merry-go-round where you have repeated chances to grab the brass ring. Don't allow once-in-a-lifetime opportunities to pass you by. If you are in school, savor every moment. You will never again have so much free time to devote to learning. If you are at a job, take advantage of everything your workplace offers.

Unlike a movie, life has no retakes.

RULE

3

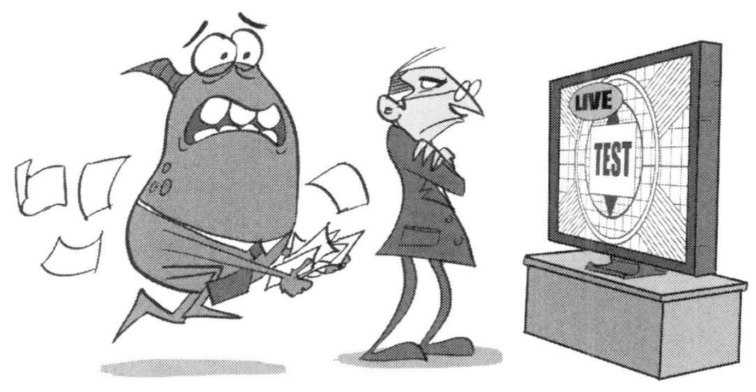

Never miss a deadline. No exceptions.

AS LONG AS there have been college assignments, students have turned in their work late. And their usual penalty is that their grade is lowered.

That is college.

In the working world, there is no lowering of a grade. There is hitting the deadline or not hitting the deadline. And people don't care why you missed the date. They just want the work finished. If you can't hit the target, they will find someone else who can.

RULE
4

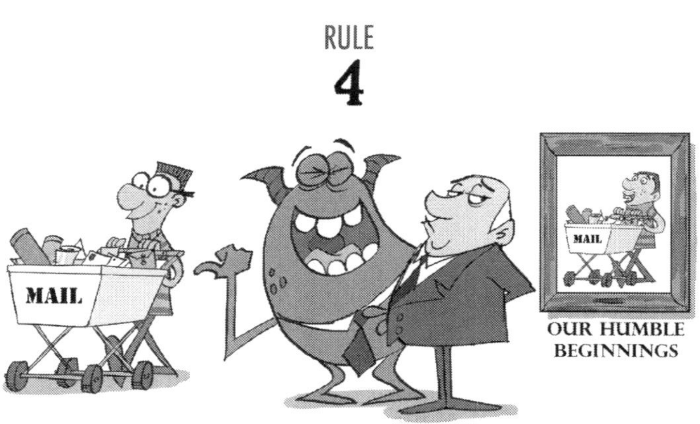

Whatever your job, do it well.

LOTS OF SUCCESSFUL people in the entertainment industry have had simple beginnings.

Before George Shapiro was the agent for comedy heavyweights Jerry Seinfeld, Carl Reiner, and Andy Kaufman, he worked in the mailroom at a talent agency. So did entertainment industry scions David Geffen, Barry Diller, and Ron Meyer. Michael Eisner, Ted Koppel, and Regis Philbin started their careers as NBC pages.

Everybody starts out at a low-level job. But smart, successful people use that job to show how good they are.

If you want to advance, follow this credo: Do your job so well that the person who follows you will have an impossible time measuring up to your standard.

RULE
5

Don't just show up. Participate.

I WENT TO a series of meetings with a well-known film personality, and at each gathering, the number of people varied. His collaborator told me why: "He doesn't like it when people don't talk in a meeting. If they don't contribute, they don't get asked back."

If you don't participate in meetings, there is no reason for you to attend. Participate and offer ideas. Your suggestion may not be the one that is implemented, but it might be the piece of information that leads to the eventual solution.

Contributing to meetings is a chance for you to demonstrate your knowledge of the subject, that you have done your homework, and that you are interested in helping the company.

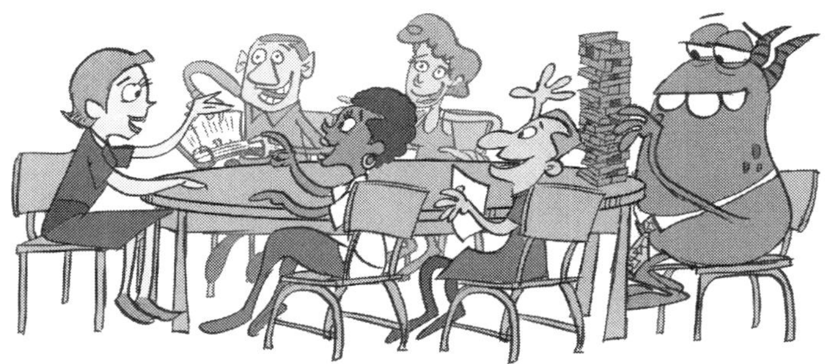

RULE

6

Take your own notes.

AT ALMOST EVERY DreamWorks meeting, a production assistant is assigned to take notes to distribute later. But I always take my own notes, too. Why?

Because I don't want the information go through someone else's filter.

I want to be clear on the course of action, and the best way to ensure that I implement the ideas correctly is to take my own notes. I also find it useful to make small sketches whenever a composition, character attitude, or idea comes to me. Those drawing notations will never appear in the meeting's typed notes.

As a rule, the notes taken by a person assigned to a meeting will be of general use to everyone who attended—but will not be specific to *you.* Make a habit of taking your own notes, and you will prevent later misunderstandings.

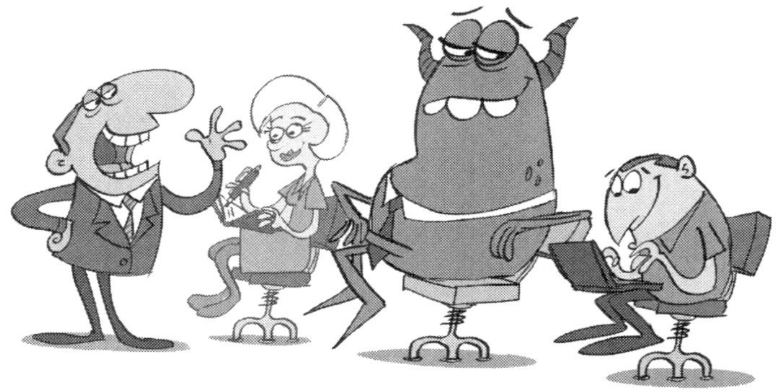

RULE

7

Proof your work.

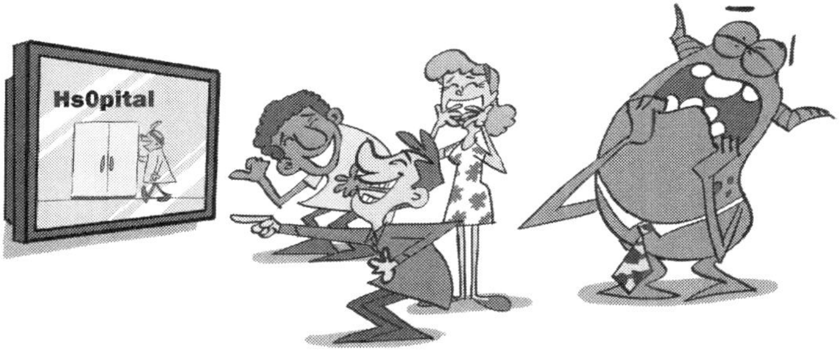

CASE STUDY: DEVELOPING a new animated movie, the filmmakers had decided on a well-known talent to play a pivotal role. They took a line of dialogue from one of the actor's previous movies and assigned their best animator to animate to the voice. Once they had their terrific sales tool, they set up a meeting with the actor to convince him to join the movie.

Seeing an animated character speaking with your voice is a big buzz for an actor, and the success rate is high in seducing actors to join projects this way. On that day, however, the actor did not get to hear his voice coming from the beautifully crafted animation scene—because the test was absolutely *silent.* No one had checked to make sure the clip had sound. The effort spent creating the test was wasted because the person responsible for getting the test to the meeting did not proof the work.

Don't put yourself in the position of: "I won't make that mistake again." Don't make it the first time. Check your work.

RULE

8

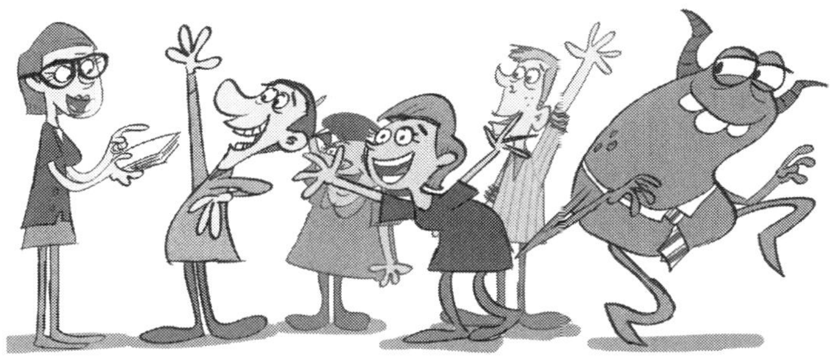

Volunteer.

THROUGHOUT MY CAREER, I have made it a policy to volunteer whenever I hear about an interesting project at my workplace. More often than not, my enthusiasm has led to some wonderful assignments.

I was once asked to help direct the voice actors for a theme park show, and I enjoyed the experience so much that I volunteered to assist on similar projects. I have since been asked to work on several DreamWorks's location-based entertainment projects, which I have enjoyed because I love theme parks.

Keep alert to the happenings at your company, and step forward to help if you hear about an interesting development. If you are offered the break, take it—and perform your task with enthusiasm.

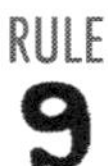

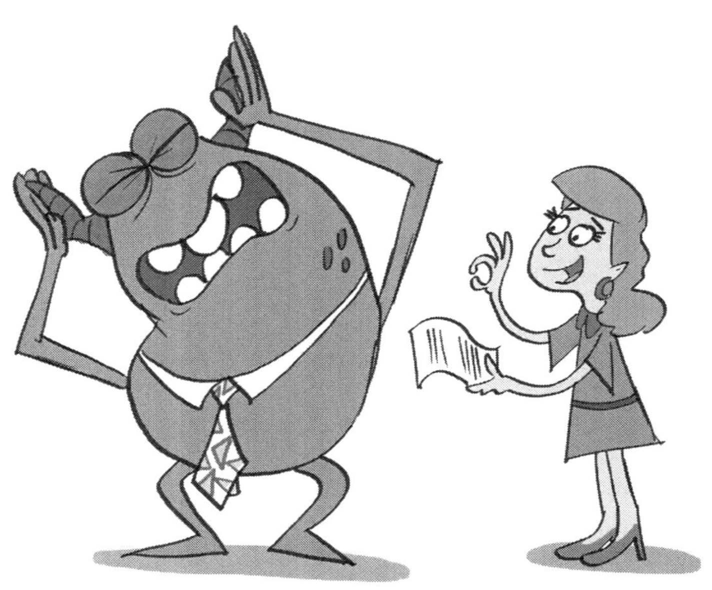

Welcome constructive criticism.

SOLICIT CONSTRUCTIVE CRITICISM about your work at every opportunity. The day you start asking people for their input is the day you start maturing as an artist. There is no time in the process that is too early or too late to consider great ideas.

Even when a film is complete, directors solicit criticism via audience previews of the film. The famous scene in *Jaws* where Hooper (Richard Dreyfuss) comes across the dead body of Ben Gardner was shot in the editor's swimming pool after Spielberg got the idea to add it during an audience preview. If Spielberg had thought it was too late to revise his work, cinema would be without one of the great "jumping out of your seat" moments.

RULE

10

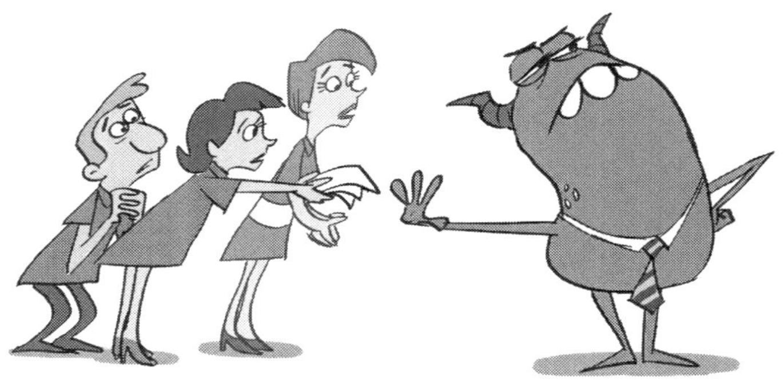

Be a great collaborator.

HANS ZIMMER, THE great film composer, is the perfect collaborator. When he was composing the score for *The Prince of Egypt,* Zimmer welcomed one of the film's directors, Simon Wells, into his studio to help him find the melody for a difficult section of the movie.

Become a better collaborator by seeking input on your work early in the process. Some of the strongest talents practice this approach and they attract a big following by creating a wonderful working experience.

If you cultivate a reputation as being someone who collaborates well, you will find yourself surrounded by the best talent.

RULE

11

Be a great teammate.

2,632. THAT'S HOW many games Cal Ripken, Jr. played in a row. Sixteen years without missing a start. How's that for being there for your teammates?

Daniel Day Lewis learned how to build a canoe for *Last of the Mohicans*. He took lessons to be a butcher for *Gangs of New York*. And constructed the house he lived in for *The Crucible*. He commits to a job and is ready for work.

You know that old commercial, "Nobody doesn't like Sara Lee"? That sentiment also goes for Betty White. She makes every project that she contributes to better—and she helps puppies in her free time. How can anyone not like her?

Being dependable, prepared, and likeable is within

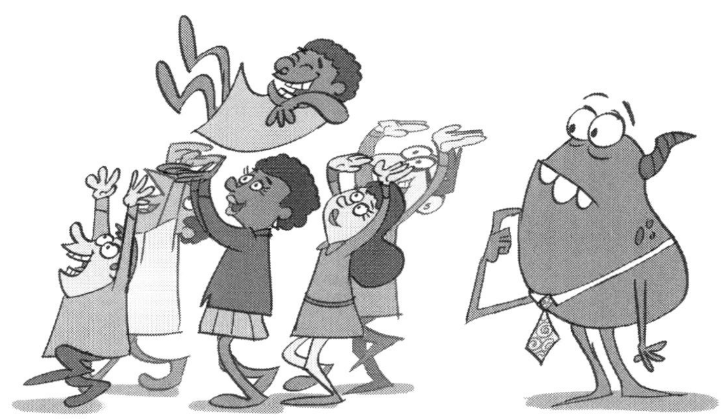

the grasp of everyone. We don't need exceptional intelligence, divine talent, or supreme good looks. We just need to commit to showing up, doing our prep work, and getting along with others. Starting today, follow these three traits, and take your first step towards being a valuable team member.

At the end of every movie is a long list of the people who contributed to creating it. It's a lot easier to make a better product—and have more fun while doing it—if everyone works as part of the team.

RULE

12

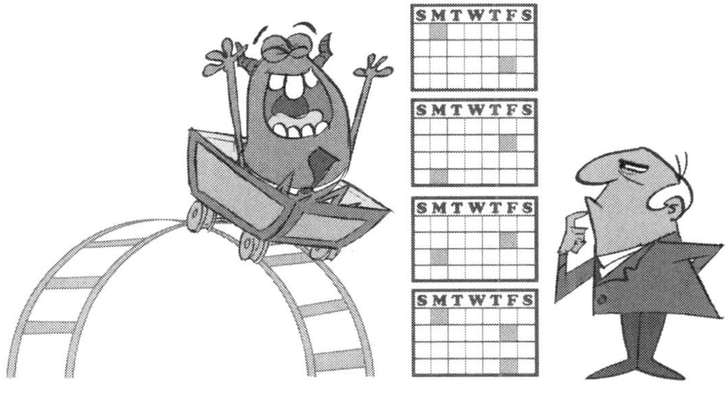

Use sick days for when you're sick.

A NEW CREWMEMBER was added to a key position, and as soon as his name was mentioned, one of the production personnel rolled his eyes. When asked what was wrong with this crewmember, the production person replied: "He always calls in sick either the Friday or the Monday after we complete a deadline. It never fails."

Sure enough, the first time we had a Thursday deadline, he was "sick" the following day. Over the length of the movie, he used all his sick days—and every one of them was called in on a Friday or a Monday after an assignment finished.

He got away with that trick for two movies before he was finally laid off.

If you repeatedly call in sick Mondays and/

or Fridays, don't be surprised if you get a reputation for it. Then you'll have all your Mondays and Fridays free.

RULE

13

"Some for the meals. Some for the reels."

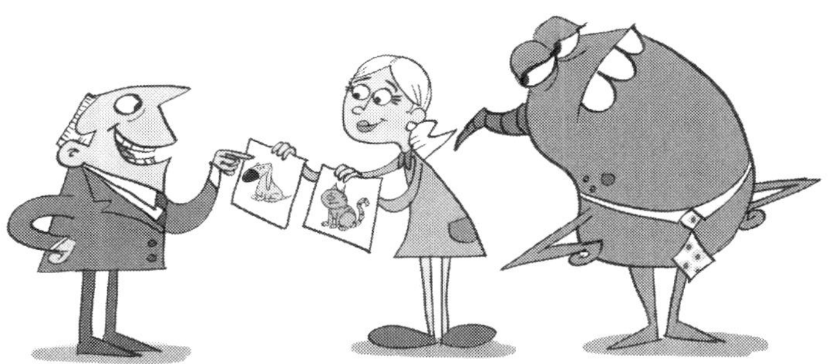

THERE'S A TRADE-OFF that artists have to make: sometimes you work on a project because it pays well, and sometimes you do it for the artistic satisfaction. (The "reel" is the demo reel that artists show to get future work.)

There are times when an artist can be given an assignment, and in the process of working the idea, thinks of an alternative solution. Often, the artist will execute the original idea and will work up his/her new suggestion. (The original idea should always be finished first—just in case the director/client doesn't care for the alternate idea.)

When you have worked up two ideas, say this before you present your work: "I did the assignment the way you suggested, and I also worked up an alternative idea that I'd like you to see."

Over the years, I have seen many alternative ideas, and I usually prefer those. I think the reason is because the second idea is an iteration of the original concept. While working on the original brief, the artist discovers a better solution.

Always execute your brief as instructed—but don't be afraid to go that extra distance and offer up an idea of your own. Who knows? That little addition might end up on your next show reel.

PART TWO

Portfolios, Presentations, and Pitches

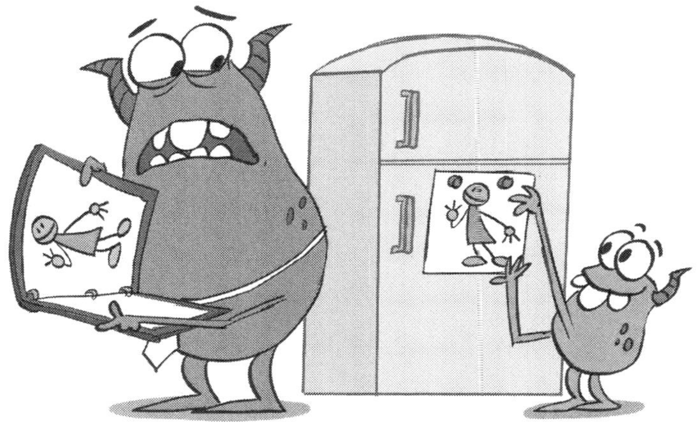

RULE

14

Don't give them a reason to put your portfolio down.

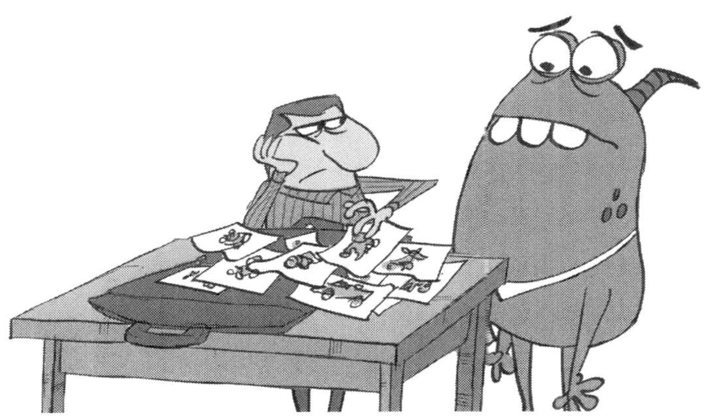

WHEN DISNEY ANNOUNCED that it would create a Los Angeles unit to handle some of the overflow work on *Who Framed Roger Rabbit?*, the office was flooded with portfolios. Feeling overwhelmed as I looked at the stacks of submissions, I knew we needed to whittle the pile down to the best ones as quickly as possible.

When you have that many portfolios to review, any inconvenience can kill an applicant's chances. No contact information? Gone. Bad photocopies of the artwork? Gone. Poorly organized? Gone.

I have even heard of a "portfolio" that consisted of a box of painted rocks—huge rocks. Don't try this!

Nobody is going to risk getting a hernia just to look at your portfolio.

Keep them turning the pages to get them more invested in your work. Present your artwork in the best possible fashion. Don't cram too many images on one page. Organize your pieces with a sense of flow. Make sure your name and contact information is easy to locate and read.

Make the experience of looking at your work fun, and you will increase your chances of getting the job.

RULE

15

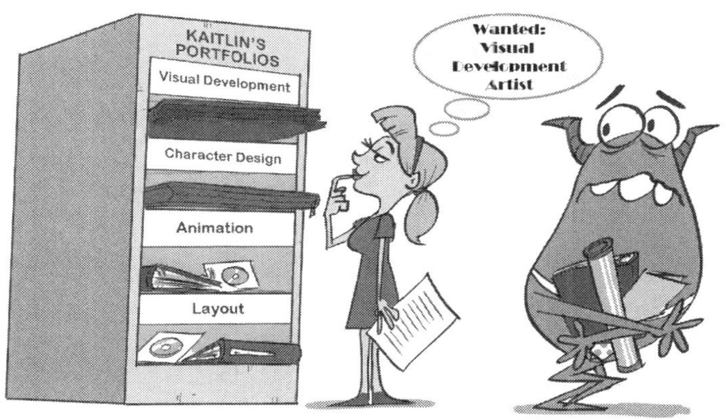

Tailor your portfolio to the job.

THERE IS NO such thing as a "One Size Fits All" portfolio.

Each submission must be specific to the job you are applying for. In animation, a Visual Development portfolio will be different from a Storyboard portfolio.

You don't have to create all new artwork for every version of your portfolio, but the *focus* of the portfolio should be different for each submission. For example, a Character Design portfolio may include some of the same pieces as a Visual Development portfolio, but it will have more emphasis on character work. It should demonstrate that you understand shapes and silhouettes, so you might design many versions of a character showing the difference in their overall shapes. A Visual Development portfolio, on the other hand, should demonstrate that you can create environments and communicate storytelling with your artwork.

Every department has its own identity. Submit the right portfolio for the job.

RULE
16

Keep your portfolio up to date.

UNEXPECTED OPPORTUNITIES ARISE and you want to be ready when they appear. I recall a situation when one studio hit it big with a movie, and suddenly they were looking to expand their slate of films. Within six months, five artists switched studios; none of them had considered leaving their present jobs until they learned about the new opportunities at the burgeoning studio. These artists weren't looking for work—the work came looking for them. But they all had current portfolios at the ready.

The window of opportunity can open and close quickly. Don't miss a terrific career chance. You never know when you are going to need to show your work. Always be prepared with an up-to-date portfolio.

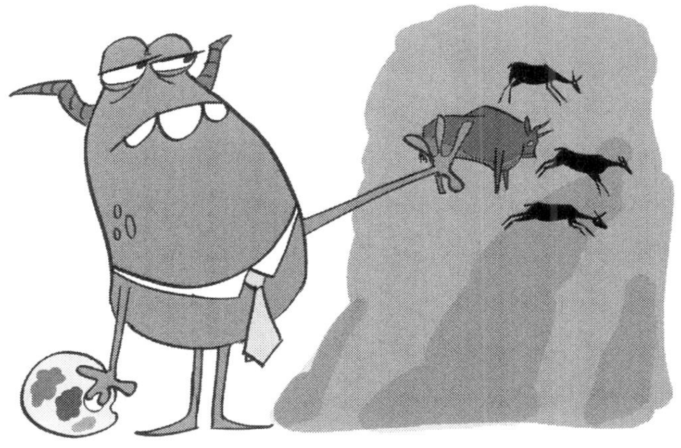

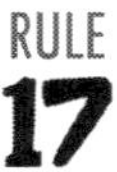

RULE 17

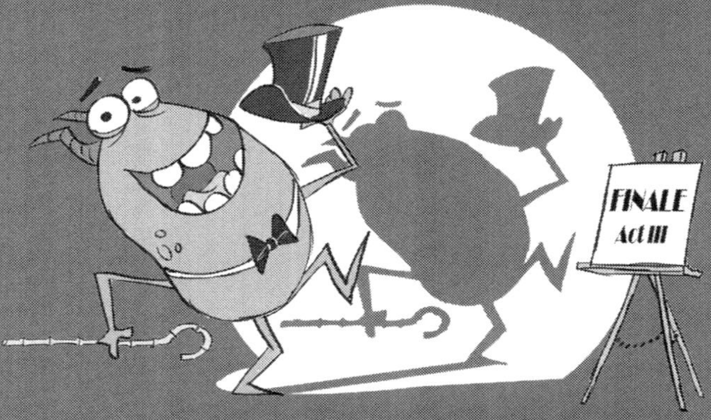

**Open strong.
Close stronger.**

ADVICE FOR ARRANGING artwork in your portfolio: Put your second-best piece of artwork first and your best piece last.

Remember rule 14, "Don't give them a reason to put your portfolio down"? By putting your second-best piece of artwork first, you ensure that the reviewer is going to immediately see some of your strength.

Putting your finest piece of artwork last leaves the reviewer with your best impression. The portfolio is a show—you want to have a great opening for your story, and an even better ending.

Choosing those first and last images is critical. Select a few of your favorites and then show them to a group of friends. Let them vote on the pieces, and whichever ones get the highest grades, put them in the opening and closing spots.

Dickens's novel, *A Tale of Two Cities*, opens with: "It was the best of times, it was the worst of times..." and closes with: "It is a far, far better thing that I do, than I have ever done...." With an opening and closing as memorable as those lines, it must be a pretty good book.

RULE

18

Keep it short.

I SAW COMEDIAN and filmmaker Jerry Lewis at the Motion Picture Academy. He was a wonderful speaker and gave one of the best filmmaking talks that I have ever heard. When he finished his presentation, he fielded some questions from the audience. After a few minutes, even though there were still many people with questions, he wrapped up the evening. Lewis said, "I was always told that it is better to leave the audience wanting than satiated."

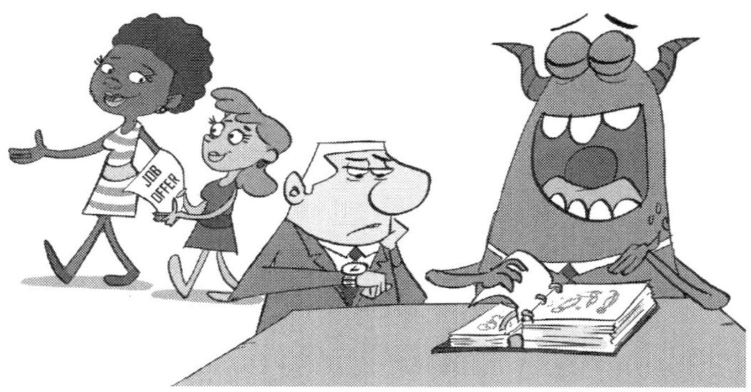

What goes for public speaking is true for portfolios and demo reels. Keep your portfolio short—you don't want to have only five pages, but you don't want fifty, either. Create a portfolio that can be casually reviewed in about five minutes. If they are engaged, they will take longer to view it, and if they want to see more, they'll ask for it. Keep demo reels between two and three minutes. No one has the time to run through your entire filmography.

Make sure your portfolio or demo reel is well edited and concise. Remove any weak links. A portfolio with one piece that is significantly weaker than the others raises a big red flag. Can't the artist distinguish between good work and bad? The artist's whole thinking process comes into question.

Be ruthless and cut anything that might be considered less than your best effort. If you have any doubt about a piece, enlist a trusted professional or friend to give you an opinion.

People make decisions on artwork surprisingly fast, and giving them too much to labor through will not increase your chances. Make it short and spectacular.

RULE

19

Learn how to make a pitch.

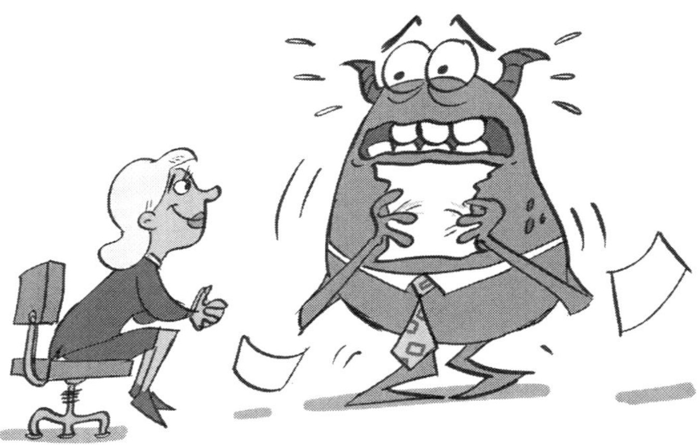

ANYONE WHO SAW Conrad Vernon pitch his storyboards for Puss in Boots' entrance in *Shrek 2* remembers it. Likewise, Tom McGrath's penguin plane crash for *Madagascar 2*. These were not routine storyboard presentations—they were perfect slices of theater.

If you are great at presenting your work, you have a huge advantage. The need to sell yourself and your work is important in entertainment, and executives and producers are swayed by dynamic personalities.

Some artists are natural performers. They love being in front of people and are good at it. But there are a lot of artists who are introverts, and they prefer expressing themselves in their artwork.

Some artists take acting lessons to improve their presentation skills. At DreamWorks, a group meets weekly as part of Toastmasters, and another group of artists does improvisational comedy.

Learn how to pitch your work—a first-rate sales pitch can make a good proposal irresistible.

RULE

20

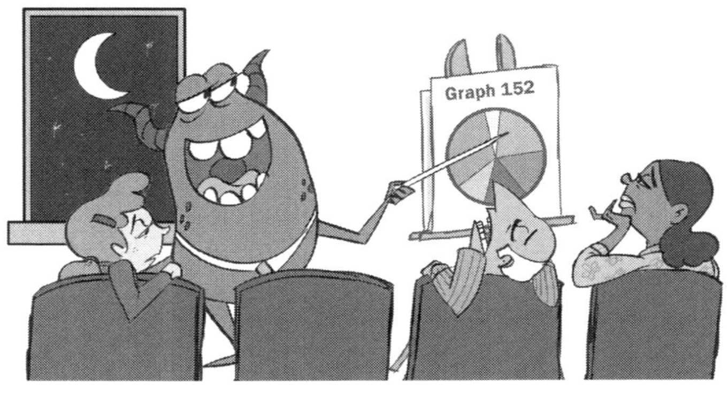

Edit your pitch.

I ONCE MADE a huge mistake when pitching an idea to Jeffrey Katzenberg. At first glance, my co-presenter and I had done everything right. We fleshed out our story, created impressive artwork, rehearsed our presentation. But we made one massive rookie blunder.

We didn't cut it down.

Our pitch ran thirty minutes—which is not necessarily too long for a pitch, but is much too long for a first pitch of a project. We went too far into the details. We were at an early stage of the project and all we needed was a response of: "Yes, this is interesting," or "No, I don't see this as a feature film." A fifteen-minute presentation would have sufficed.

Luckily, the studio was already considering the

project so we didn't kill the project with our misstep, but I learned the vital lesson to respect the audience's time.

RULE

21

Make your pitch bulletproof.

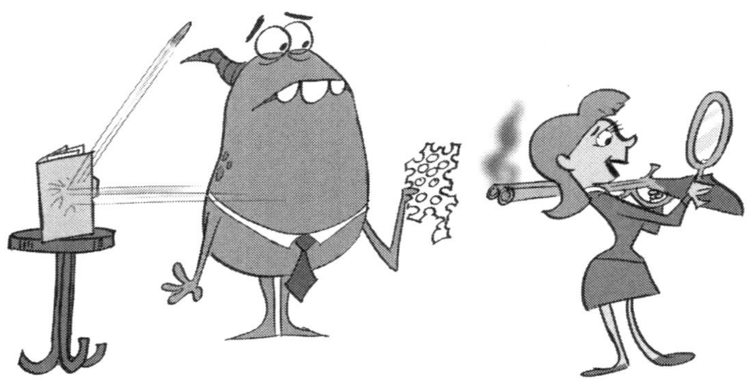

DURING THE MAKING of *Bee Movie*, we created a joke version of the movie as a theater teaser trailer. Jerry Seinfeld, in a bee costume, and Chris Rock, in a mosquito costume, reenacted a scene from the movie as a live action film—to disastrous results. Then Steven Spielberg entered, reviewed the failed footage, and proclaimed, "Let's make it a cartoon."

On the day of the shooting, I was amazed at Seinfeld's level of concentration. He and Rock were being thrown about by giant windshield wipers and sprayed with water, yet they always managed to deliver their jokes perfectly.

I have pitched storyboard sequences, movie ideas, and scripts hundreds of times in my career, but I still get nervous beforehand. I asked Seinfeld how he managed to stay focused and not forget his lines. He told me that whenever you get in front of the camera or a group of people, there will be distractions. The best way to prevent mistakes is to over-prepare.

He suggested that for my upcoming presentation, I learn my words backwards and forwards to make my presentation bulletproof. I made sure that I had extensive rehearsal to leave nothing to chance.

The antidote to having nerves "on the day" is to over-prepare.

RULE

22

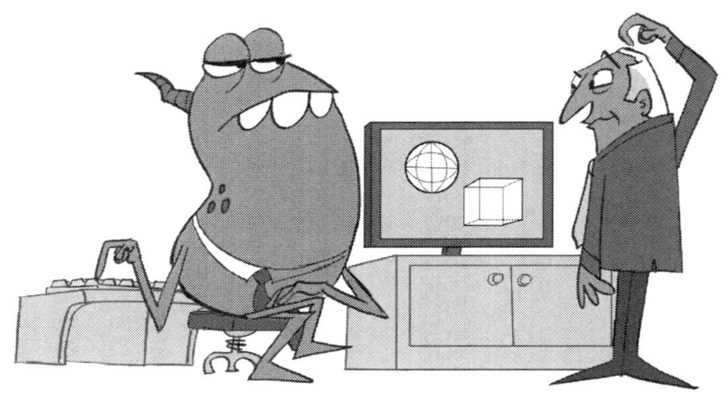

Set up your work.

ONE OF THE most common mistakes artists make is not providing the context for their work before they present it. While the artist has been consumed by his/her piece of the project, the executives, producers, or director(s) may need to be reminded how that precise piece fits into the larger scheme.

A typical presentation may occur like this: Jeffrey Katzenberg comes into a room to see how the visual effects development is shaping up on a movie. The effects animator, forgetting that Katzenberg has spent the past two weeks working on theme parks, television shows, other movies, staged entertainment, board meetings, and outside philanthropic concerns, says, "Here's an idea for an explosion," and hits the *play* button. Katzenberg sees three animated explosions on the movie screen and is expected to comment—but he has no idea what the explosion is about or why it is even in the story. The artist did not provide Katzenberg with any context to evaluate the scene.

This is how that presentation should have occurred: The artist explains that he is working on the explosions for the villain character's "smart bomb" for the sequence at the end of Act Two—where the villain wipes out the guards, but leaves the structure standing so he doesn't destroy the valuable item he is seeking. The artist then explains that he will be showing three different versions of the explosions; some with more fire but less smoke and some with more smoke but less fire.

Now, Katzenberg understands the purpose for the explosion effects. The review of the effects work can be productive instead of just a random screening of explosions.

If the review is to see adjustments from a previous presentation, the artist needs to reiterate what the original note was and how he/she has corrected the work. The artist must remind the supervisor, director, producer, or executive why they are seeing the work again, and what precisely has been changed. Remember, your goal is to get your work approved, and the best way to do that is by making sure everyone is clear why the change was requested and what you have done to correct it.

PART THREE

Improve Yourself

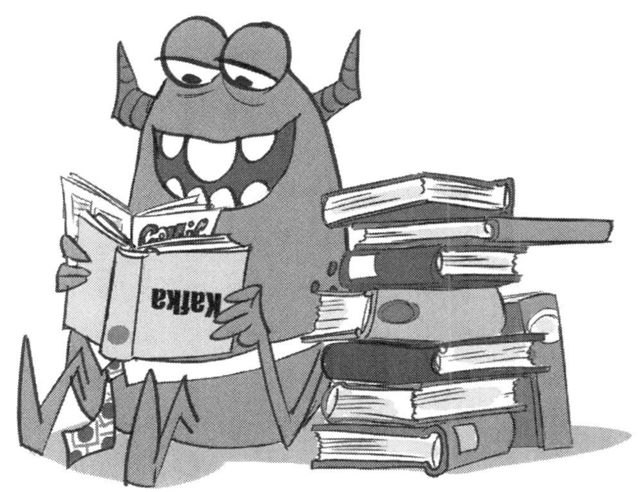

RULE

23

Be better than average.

ON MY FIRST day of film school at New York University, one fact was clear: each person in the room was the probably best filmmaker in his/her high school. I might have been the best in my school, but in this crowd, I was only average.

When I made it to Disney Studios, it happened again. The artists around me were the best from their colleges. I was among the best animators in my college, but here I was only average.

At DreamWorks, we have artists from all over the world. Some of the artists working alongside me are the best in their *country*. The standard for what constitutes "average" is higher than ever.

At Pixar, Disney, Blue Sky, Illumination, Laika,

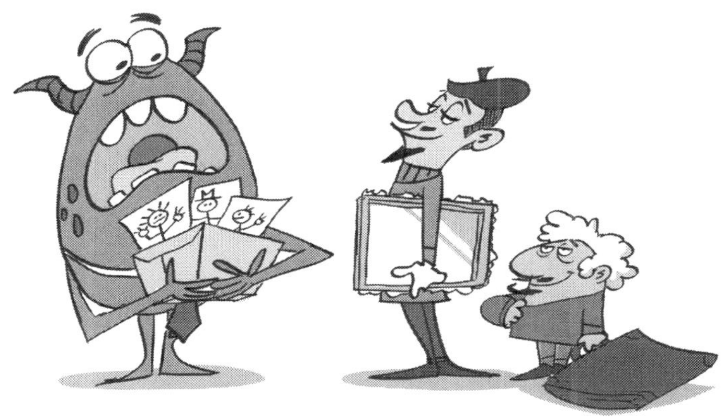

Sony, and DreamWorks, the same high level of "average" occurs. Everybody's great when you get to the highest level. There is no room for your B game.

RULE

24

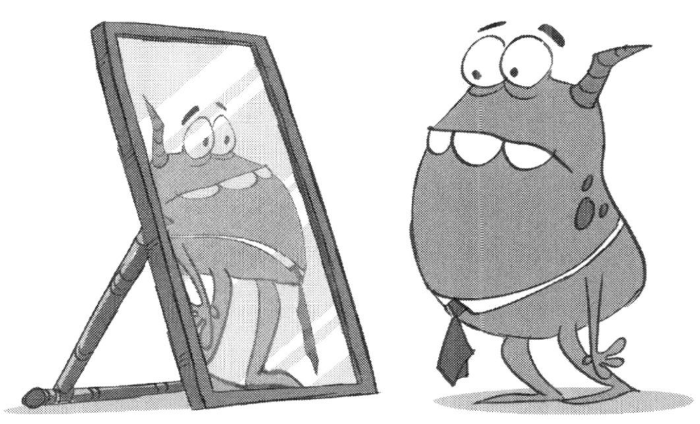

Be in competition with yourself.

THE TALENT POOL is deep in the entertainment business, but I don't consider the other artists to be my competition. My philosophy is that I am not in competition with other artists—I am in competition with myself. My goal is to become the best version of myself.

I can't control the talent or ability level of other artists, but I can control my own ability. I can adjust my skills and improve myself. I don't waste my energy fretting over another person's opportunities—if they succeed, good for them. I analyze why that artist is doing well and try to acquire that skill.

Take ownership of your career and vow to be the best version of you. And always view yourself as a work in progress.

STEVE HICKNER

RULE

25

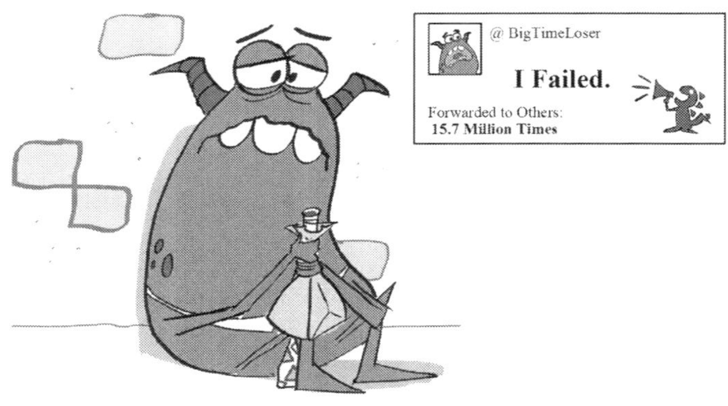

Everyone fails.

BILL GATES'S FIRST business, Traf-O-Data, failed. Stephen King's bestseller *Carrie* was rejected by thirty publishers. Sir James Dyson went through 5,126 failed prototypes before he made a vacuum cleaner that worked.

My own failures were much less spectacular, but they still stung. I was removed from my first storyboard job after one month. And I have a sheaf of studio rejection letters from my early days in Los Angeles.

Don't take it personally. You will fail at some point.

But failure does not have to be permanent. What matters is how quickly you recover.

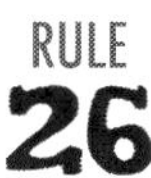

RULE 26

Learn from people at the top.

PEOPLE REACH THE top of their professions because they have special talents and skills for working with others. When you work with top people, observe what makes them successful and learn from them.

From Robert Watts (producer on the original *Star Wars* trilogy), I learned the value of making everyone you speak to feel important. From Don Hahn (producer of *The Lion King* and *Beauty and the Beast*), I learned the importance of walking the floor and connecting with every artist. From Robert Zemeckis (director of *Forrest Gump* and *Back to the Future*), I learned that you can't have greatness without a team. From Jeffrey Katzenberg (former chairman of Walt Disney Studios and current CEO of DreamWorks Animation), I learned that there is no substitute for returning phone calls, e-mails, messages, and being the first one into the office. From Steven Spielberg

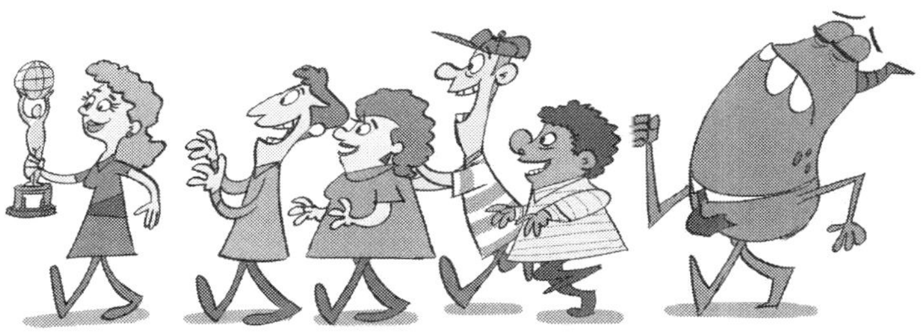

(director and co-founder of DreamWorks Studio), I learned what genius looks like and how to inspire. And from Jerry Seinfeld (comedian, actor, and writer/director), I learned that laughing and doing great work can be one and the same.

Every day I try to emulate the skills of the very best in the business with whom I have had the privilege to work. If you're lucky enough to find yourself with top people, understand what makes them great and learn.

RULE

27

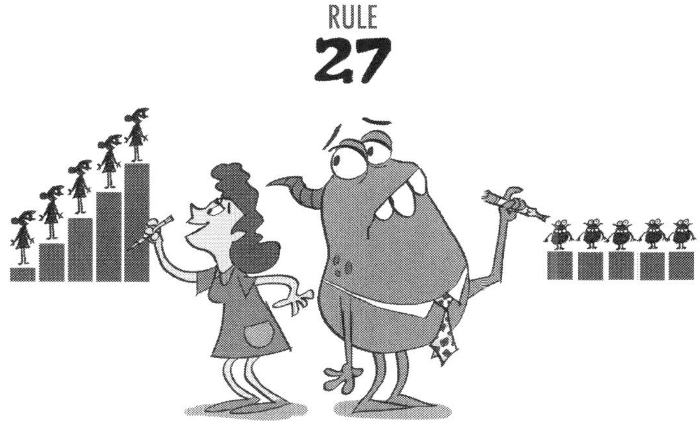

Learn something new every year.

"WHEN LIFE GIVES you lemons..." It's an old expression, but, by following this advice, I have been able to make some lemonade.

One year, after working on a frustrating project, I felt that I had not learned anything new. I enrolled in a Photoshop class to pick up some new tricks. The class was exhilarating. By the end of the weekend, I was excited to get back to work and apply my new knowledge.

Then I signed up for an editing class and learned how to use a digital editing machine. After that, I took a computer animation class. I was the worst student in the room, but I didn't care. I was hooked.

By taking those classes in the final weeks of what had seemed like a lost year, I ended the year on a high point, with a whole toolbox of new skills. I now look back on that frustrating project with gratitude, because it led me to the realization that I needed to learn something new every year.

Take a class. Pick up a new trick or two. Make the resolution to end every year with (at least) one more skill than you had at the beginning.

RULE

28

Be a student of your field.

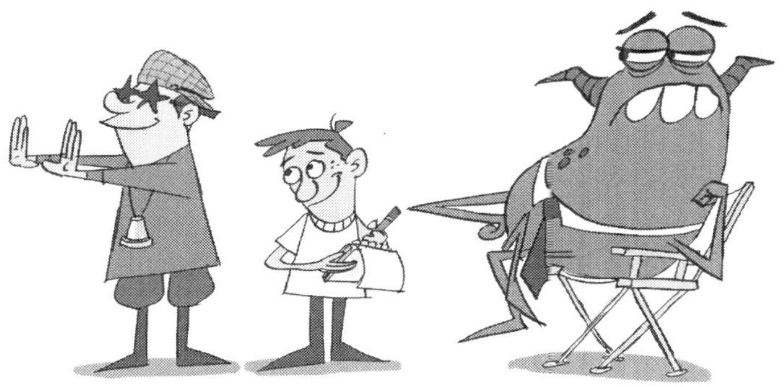

THE MOVIEMAKERS OF the past and present are such an inspiration for me that I am bewildered when I visit film schools and find that many of the students don't seem to be curious about the artists who preceded them.

I read an interview (*Lab Magazine*, July 10, 2010) with the character actor Tim Blake Nelson (*O Brother, Where Art Thou?*, *Hoot*, *Lincoln*) who said it well: "You are not an artist without a sense of tradition."

Great artists build on the foundation of their predecessors. Achieving excellence without studying the founders of your specialization is not possible. Be a student of your field.

RULE

29

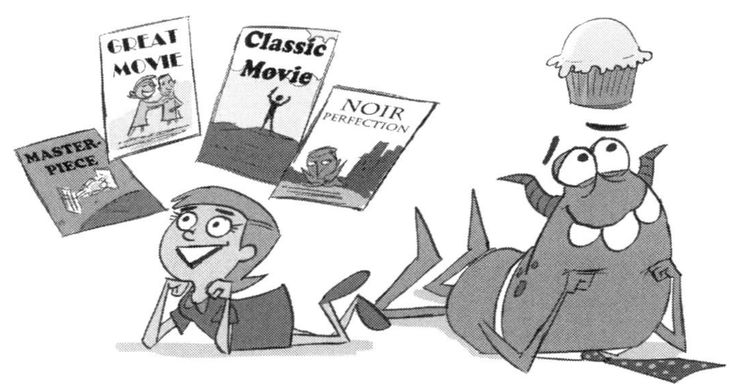

Immerse yourself in inspiration.

ONE OF THE first things that animation director Richard Williams did when he started work on *Who Framed Roger Rabbit?* was to create a huge board of 1930s and 1940s animated characters. He wanted to surround himself with examples from the world that he was trying to re-create.

When layout artist Mike Peraza was designing a sequence inside London's Big Ben for Disney's animated film, *The Great Mouse Detective*, he built a huge tabletop model of the famous clock tower so he could physically work in its shadow.

Check the desks of most animators. Some have action figures of The Incredibles; others have comic book covers from the Marvel Universe. Reproductions of artwork by the Great Masters are commonplace.

Although each of the artists has his/her own influences, the purpose of building an environment of creativity is the same: a source of inspiration.

Create your own cocoon of creativity.

RULE

30

Make every day a "school day."

WHENEVER I THINK that I don't have time for a movie or a reading assignment, I think about film directors Steven Spielberg and Guillermo Del Toro. Those guys see and read everything. They are lifetime learners.

Every day when I step onto my elliptical trainer, I also enter an educational zone. There is a monitor in front of me to view contemporary, classic, foreign, and documentary films. (I watched all 180 episodes of *Seinfeld* on my elliptical machine while we were making *Bee Movie*).

The iPad extends my reach of learning experiences while I'm traveling, and even in the backyard. With just a swipe of my finger, I can pull up articles, blogs, and opinion pieces that are topical or archived. When the Telluride, Sundance, or Cannes film festivals take place, I feel connected.

But the resource that ensures I will be a lifetime film student is the vast cyber-warehouse of material on YouTube. While I'm drawing, I listen to interviews with film directors Alfred Hitchcock, Frank Capra, John Ford, Martin Scorsese, Steven Spielberg, George Lucas, Quentin Tarantino, Chris Nolan, and others. I've heard talks with Groucho Marx, Cary Grant, Stan Laurel, and Orson Welles. TED talks

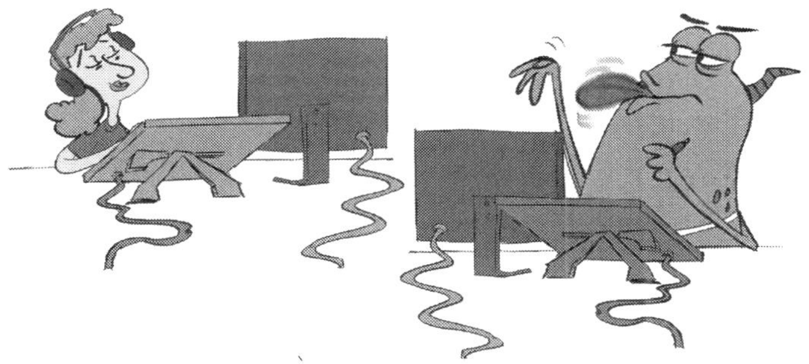

alone have kept me occupied for weeks.

The wealth of available material is almost unimaginable, and provides us with a chance to continue our education on a daily basis. For the cost of Internet service or a Netflix membership, you can step into the classrooms of some of the greatest minds of every field.

Do yourself a favor—enroll today.

RULE

31

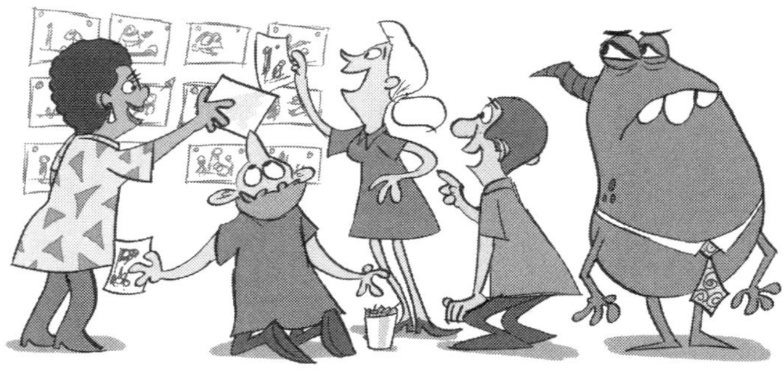

Surround yourself with people who love their jobs.

MY FIRST JOB in the animation business involved working with all the animators in the studio, and in the course of my workday I would visit their offices. One room had two animators who loved everything about animation. Each time I approached their office, I could hear peals of laughter. They told me great stories about working at other studios, and it was so much fun with them, I had to drag myself back to my work.

I made the decision in those early days that I always wanted to be working in "the room with laughter." If you work around people who are having fun, then that spirit of fun spreads to you and all the others on the project.

Unfortunately, a toxic environment also spreads. There was another room that was occupied by two long-time animators who always seemed to be having a bad day. Nothing was ever right, and the scenes that they were assigned to animate were either too complicated or not challenging enough.

Avoid the people who complain. Eventually their poison will infect you. Choose your work friends carefully and spend your time with the ones who love their jobs.

RULE 32

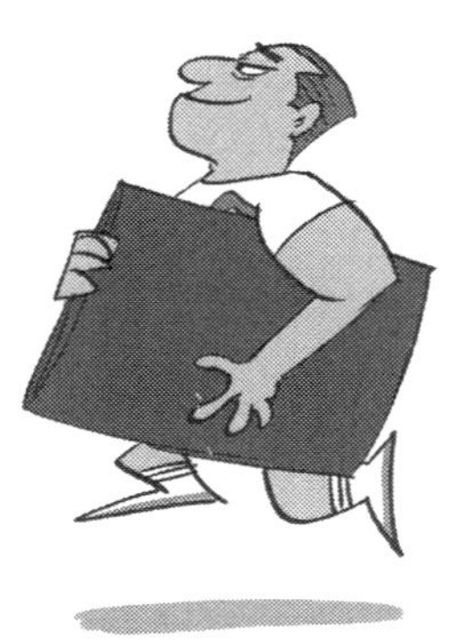

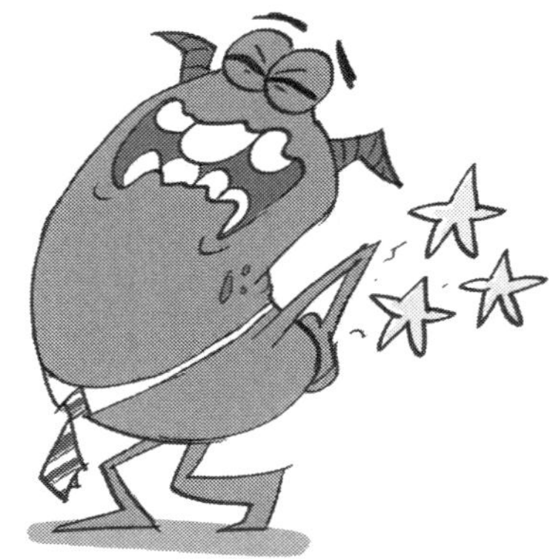

Keep in shape.

WHAT DOES HITTING the gym have to do with drawing, writing or creating? Plenty.

If your back hurts, you might not be able to draw. If you have tendonitis, you might not be able to type. And if your energy level is low, your creativity suffers.

As you get older, staying fit makes a big difference. If you have a health problem, you might not be able to work. And if you aren't working, you aren't making money.

If you spend your day at a computer or drawing board, it is important to get up and move around periodically. Develop good health habits so you can keep working as long as you want to.

PART FOUR

Cold Hard Truths

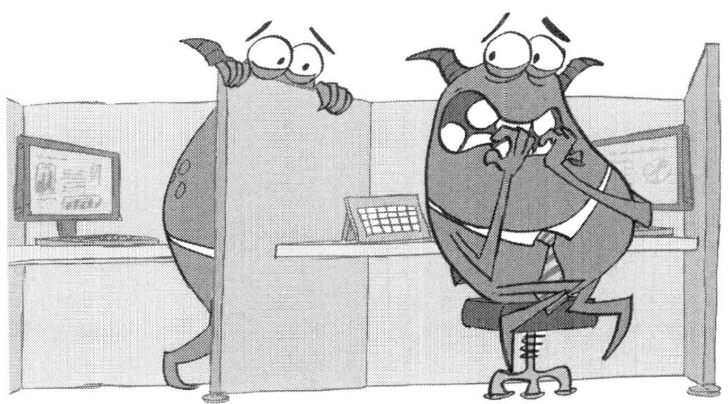

RULE

33

It's a small world.

WHEN I WAS directing *The Prince of Egypt,* Bill Damaschke was hired as a production manager. Now, he is the chief creative officer for DreamWorks. I hired Mark Swift for his first job—lugging sheets of plywood up three flights of stairs. Later, Swift was one of the producers of *Bee Movie*. They both started with a low rank, but have ended up overseeing me.

There is an old adage, and it's true: "Be nice to the people on the way up, because they're the same ones you meet on the way down."

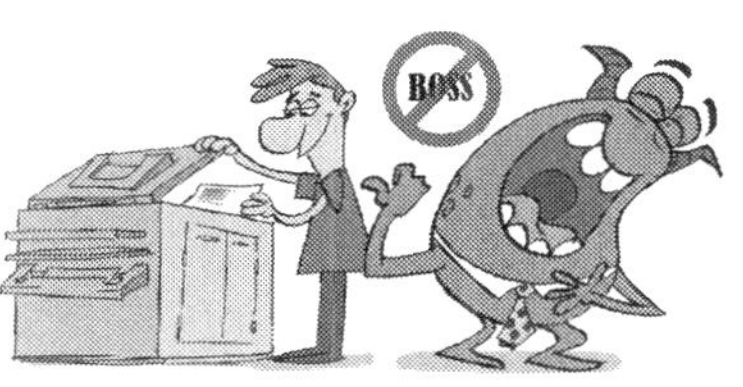

The world of entertainment is a small one. You run into the same people all the time.

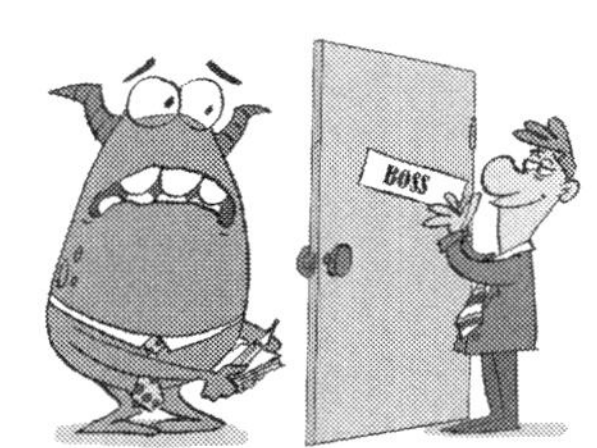

The people you are working with today will probably be at another studio/agency/company some day in the future. Be nice to them—they may be the ones hiring.

RULE 34

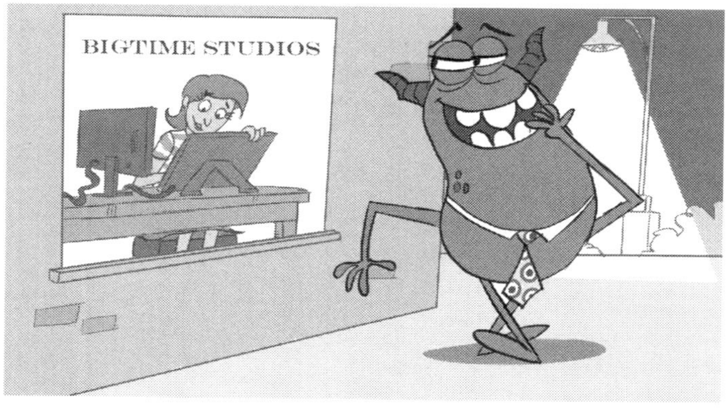

This ain't a hobby.

WHEN I TRANSFERRED into New York University film school as a sophomore, I was told that the freshman class that started the year before was enormous. By the time I graduated, there were far fewer of us in the class.

The reason so many of my fellow film students dropped out is that they entered the program under the mistaken idea that it would be fun and easy. There is no question that making movies can be fun, but creating something of quality is never easy. It takes tremendous effort to finish even a bad movie, and the field is highly competitive.

At any animation studio, you won't find many people who can claim that they have been in the animation business for ten years. Raise that bar to twenty, and the number drops off precipitously. Look for people with thirty or forty years experience and you will barely fill a small table.

The entertainment business is not a part-time job or hobby. You have to commit to it in order to be one of the few who makes it a long-time career.

RULE

35

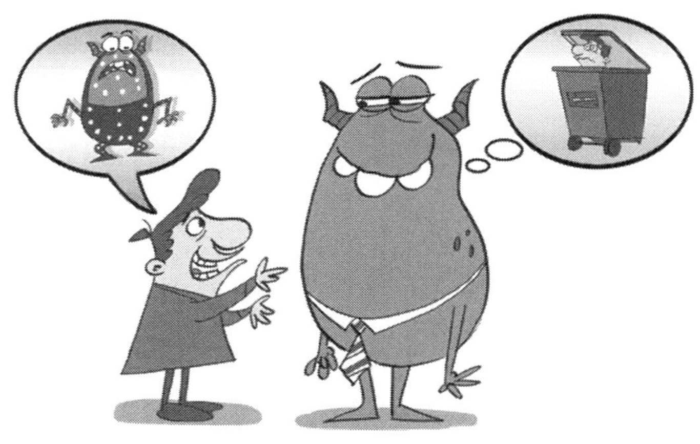

Try the new thing.

I SAW THE Los Angeles Animation Guild's (the industry's union) employment graph of the last twenty-five years, and the curve looked as if it would make a great roller coaster. There were good years (1986, 1999, 2010) and bad years (1989, 2000-2004). The boom times were coincident with major animated film successes. The bust times followed catastrophic events such as the closing of Filmation, one of the industry's biggest employers, and when Disney shuttered its hand-drawn animation department.

That graph represented the last quarter-century, but it might as well have been projecting the next two decades, because one truth is absolute: there will be good times and bad times. And the best way to ride through those future bad times is to plan for them today.

Identify the upcoming technologies and enroll in classes that teach those skills. The newest tools show up in the works of the cutting-edge directors like Peter Jackson, James Cameron, Steven Spielberg, Chris Nolan, and others, so don't miss a talked-about film. The big directors were among the first to use the pre-visualization of movies, a process that is now common in both live-action and animated films. The layout artists that embraced the technology when it was emerging stayed ahead of their peers. The motion-capture techniques from *The Lord of the Rings* and *Avatar* are now making inroads into animated features.

Be the first artist to adopt the newest technology, not the last one trying to catch up.

RULE

36

Being "transitioned off" is sometimes code for "Get rid of him (or her)."

IN THE ENTERTAINMENT business, people don't like firing artists because one day they might need them again. So, when a difficult artist becomes a liability, an unspoken—and passive-aggressive—dance takes place. Production people may avoid conflict by citing a "departmental scale-down" as the reason for the dismissal. Because the off-loading of the difficult person coincides with the end of a project, the artist may be clueless as to the reason he or she is being let go.

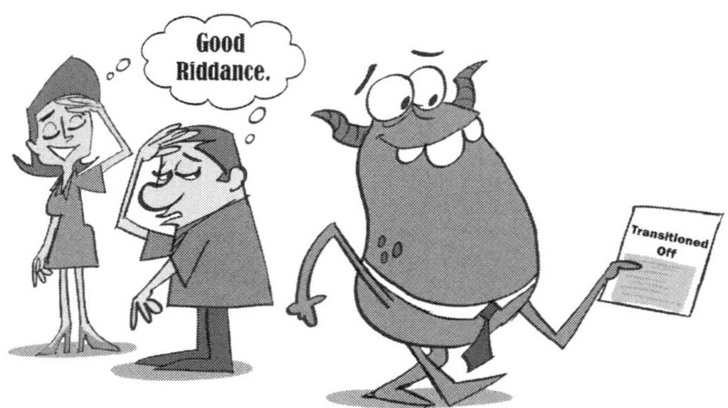

The action might look benign, but it is not. An artist who is "transitioned off" is nuked for being a nuisance.

If you are repeatedly "transitioned off" a project—while other artists in your department are retained—or you are often informed that you are a casualty of a "departmental scale-down," it may be a warning that you are regarded as a difficult employee. Such a label can be fatal, and if you don't address your behavior, you may soon find yourself unemployable.

People avoid confrontation, and trying to find someone to tell you the real reason for your dismissal will be difficult. If you are let go, ask for an exit interview or ask your boss if there is something about your performance that you could improve. If you want to uncover the truth, you will need to avoid being defensive and confrontational. From the company's viewpoint, you have already been delicately dealt with and they have no incentive to reopen the issue.

RULE

37

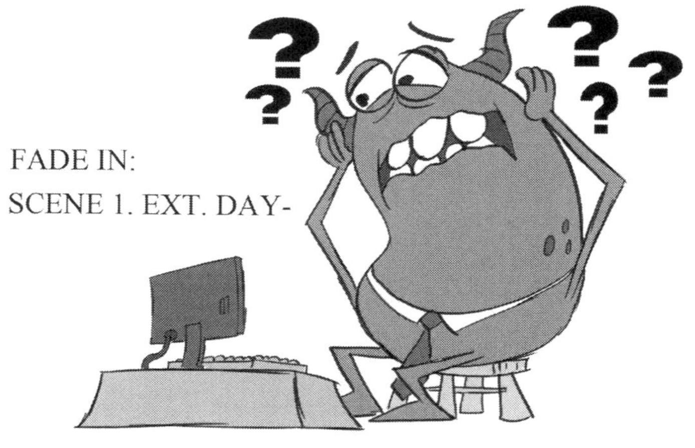

The story dilemma: What you learn on one movie won't help you with the next.

WARD KIMBALL, ONE of Disney's most valued animators, recounted many tales about his work there in a 1978 interview with Steve Hulett, which was posted on the TAG blog in 2006. The crew believed they had solved the problem of making movies after the runaway success of *Snow White and the Seven Dwarfs*. But soon after they started *Pinocchio*, they ran into difficulties. "Six months later we found out that what you learn in one picture doesn't necessarily work in the next picture."

The challenges you solve when telling a story are so specific to that narrative that they don't necessarily carry over to the next film. And here's why: because you are not telling *that* story again.

There are some aspects of what you learn in making a film that can be carried over from one movie to the next. For the most part, these are the technical aspects of moviemaking. But as Kimball learned, that doesn't seem to happen in the story department.

The two movies that I directed, *The Prince of Egypt* and *Bee Movie,* could not be more dissimilar; one is a biblical morality tale and the other is an absurd, lighthearted comedy. There is nothing that will translate from the character of Moses to Barry the Bee—both movies had different questions to answer.

Even when you make a sequel, the character will have changed from the first movie and so the character will not be the same as in the previous film.

Storytelling is not manufacturing widgets; it is a fluid process and the parts are continually moving. That's why making films is so hard—and why it's so rewarding when it works.

RULE

38

Every studio is two flops from disaster.

THIS RULE IS from Shamus Culhane, courtesy of long-time animator/animation professor, Tom Sito. Many years ago, Sito worked as Culhane's assistant and he picked up this wisdom first-hand. (Shamus Culhane is an animation legend and is known for animating many of the memorable scenes of *Snow White*.)

When a studio starts an animation film, the second film must be put into work before the first one has been released because of the long lead time and overlapping nature of animation production.

Let's say the first film flops. The studio regroups and declares it is committed to the second film. But the unspoken, dirty secret is that the studio is

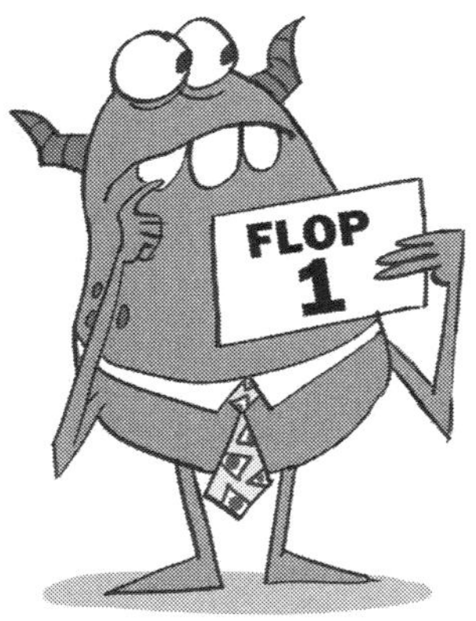

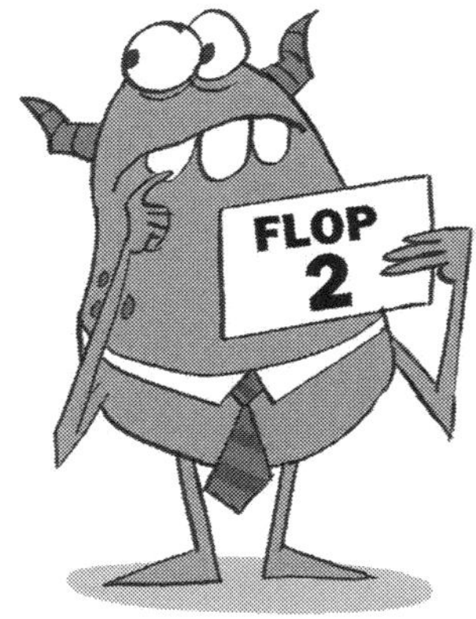

continuing with the second film only because it is already half-finished—not out of love for the movie.

After the second flop, it is time for the studio to "re-evaluate the situation." When you hear that phrase, it's time to get the portfolio ready. If you are waiting for film number three, you will be waiting a long time.

RULE

39

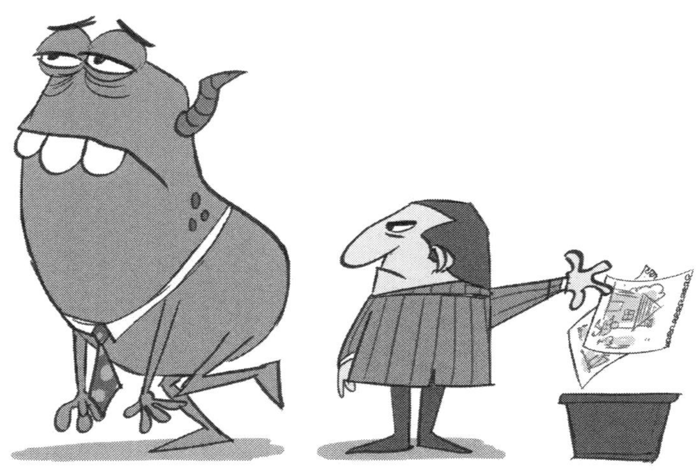

Watch for freelance erosion.

I REMEMBER A Superstar Artist who came blazing onto the scene and impressed everyone with the quality and quantity of his work. His reputation grew and other studios approached him about working for them in his free time. Seeing an opportunity to make extra money by freelancing, the Superstar Artist said, "Yes."

As the Superstar Artist began to moonlight for the other studios, everyone at the Day Job studio noticed that his output dropped. And so did his quality. The Superstar Artist's best work was reserved for the freelancing studios—because those jobs were auditions for future commissions—and the Day Job studio received his leftover efforts.

It didn't take long for the Day Job studio to realize that they could get better work—and not pay benefits like vacation and sick days—if they were to hire the Superstar Artist as a freelancer. And guess what? When the project the Superstar Artist was working on for the Day Job studio came to an end, he was laid off.

Only to be later rehired as a freelancer.

I don't recommend freelancing while working on staff. If you do, watch closely for signs of erosion in your primary job. If you sense a qualitative decline, then stop—or you will soon burn both bridges.

Your employer is paying for your best work. Make sure that's what you give.

RULE

40

"Appearing equal" is not the same as "being equal."

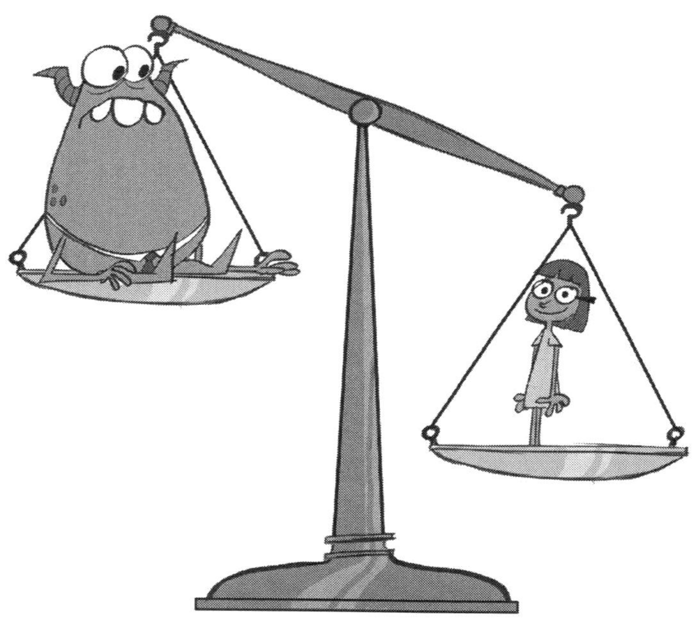

THERE WILL ALWAYS be someone who is doing the same job as you are and is making more money. But before you grind your teeth in frustration at the apparent inequality, ask yourself a few questions:

"Do I deliver my work as timely as he/she does?" "Am I as reliable?" "Is my work as good?" "Do I require less supervision?" And most importantly—"Was my last movie a huge hit while his/her film underperformed?"

If you answered "No" to any of these questions, then you are *not* doing the same job as your co-worker.

An artist who turns out great work with little supervision is worth a premium. But when it comes to salary negotiation in Hollywood, there is one attribute that trumps them all.

Box office.

Despite the enthusiasm of those trophies during award season, there is nothing better than having your project make a lot of money if you want cachet in Hollywood. A hit movie means you are worth more to people because everyone hopes your money-making "magic" will rub off on their project.

There are a million intangibles why that person may make more money than you do. Rather than obsess over the differences, channel that energy into doing your own work better.

Believe me, if your work delivers a hit, you'll get the Benjamins.

RULE

41

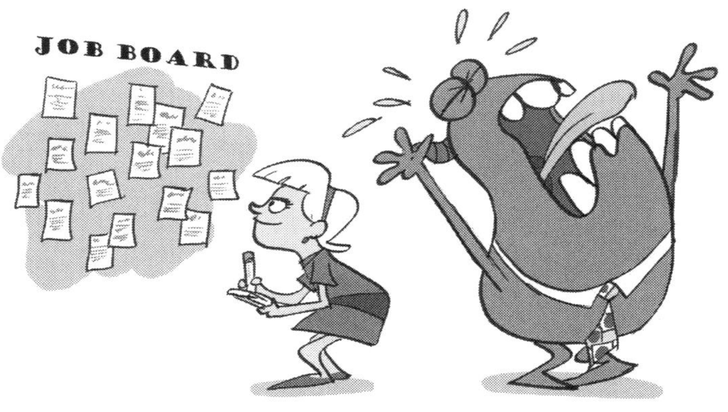

You *will* be laid off.

FIVE MONTHS. THAT'S how long it took from being hired at Filmation until being laid off. It was my first job after graduating college, and I thought that was how employment operated in the "real world." You worked for a few months, and then you were laid off.

Although I didn't enjoy looking for a new job so soon after finding one, that experience put into bold relief a vital lesson: this would not be a career with stability.

Since those early years, I have been lucky to remain employed at a series of wonderful studios. But most artists in the animation industry move from job to job with multiple studios. Even the best talents experience periods of downtime.

If you want to work as an artist, remember: at some point, you will be laid off from your job. Don't take it personally. It happens to everyone. Prepare for that moment and put away some money for the lean times—because there will be lean times.

RULE

42

Don't waste time. You will never get it back.

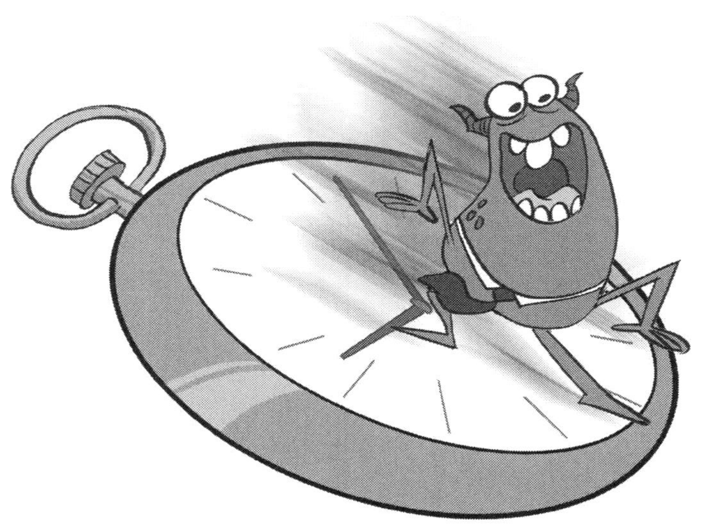

TIME IS OUR greatest commodity. None of us knows how many days we get, and to allow a single one to go to waste is a crime. In all my years in animation, the only regret I have is the time I stayed on a project when I was miserable and knew the project would implode (which it did). Only when I was on the other side of that disaster did I realize my sin of losing that time.

The gap in my filmography is my reminder of those squandered days.

I knew an artist who wanted to get into the animation business. He did everything right: took the best courses, assembled a good demo reel. But when he finished his classes, he jumped on a plane and spent an extended time enjoying himself in Europe with friends. His classmates were out in the field, hunting down their first jobs.

By the time the artist returned from his European vacation, he had lost the momentum from the classes. The peak season for television animation hiring was over, and he had missed it.

He applied for a few jobs, became discouraged, and moved to a new city to enroll in a different college program.

Time only makes withdrawals. Use each day wisely.

PART FIVE

It's a Career

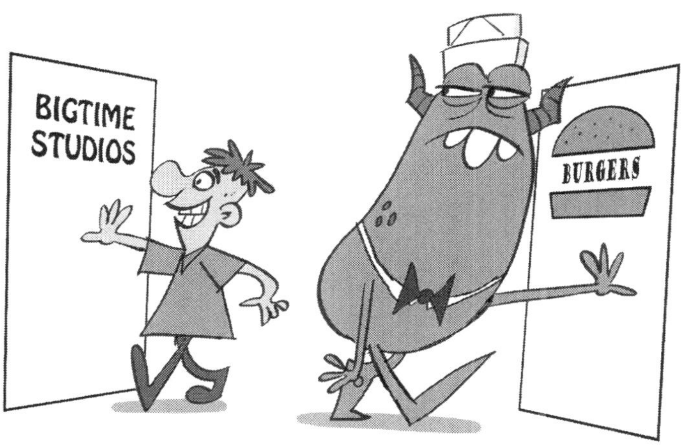

RULE

43

Give it 100 percent.

ONE DAY I was listening to a sports radio show, and the program's host asked a coach of a top-ranked college football program why he drove himself so hard. The coach responded that he only knew what 100 percent of any behavior looked like. "I don't know what 98 percent of integrity is. Is this the time that I can lie or cheat? Can I still cheat again tomorrow if I do it today? Is that still within the 98 percent? I don't know. But I know what 100 percent is."

The same goes for your work. Always commit 100 percent to every project. Don't allow some assignments to become stepchildren. If you pull back and give less than your full effort this time, will you allow yourself to do the same next time? As Vince Lombardi said, "Winning is a habit. Unfortunately, so is losing."

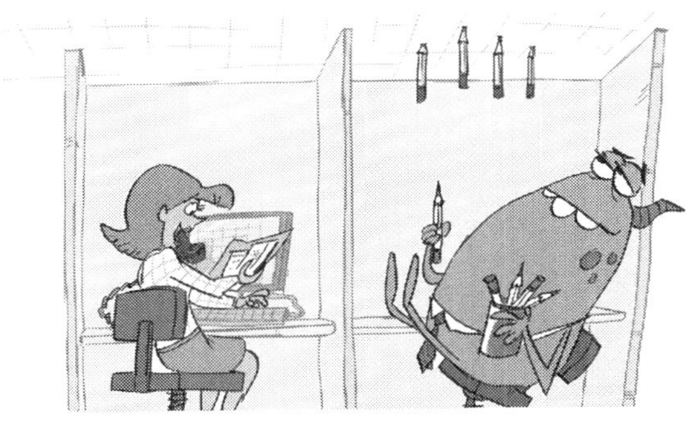

RULE
44

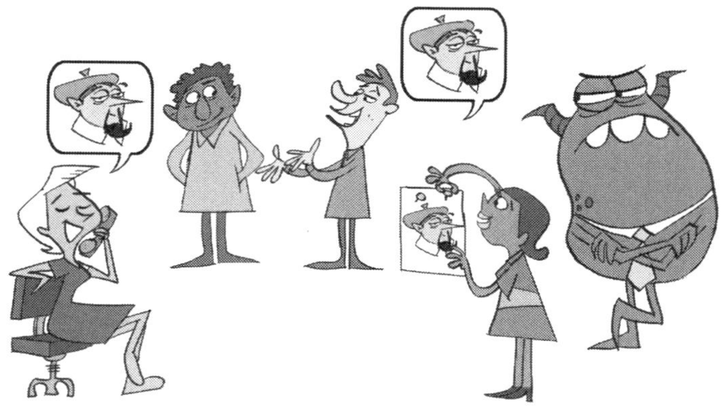

Be known for something special.

DEVELOP ONE SPECIAL skill so you can be known for doing it exceptionally well. When I think of great animation specialists, three storyboard artists come to mind. One is great at inventing funny ideas for characters to do in their scenes (we call this "business"). Another artist is terrific at musical numbers. And the third artist is without peer when it comes to action sequences. These three talented people can storyboard anything, but they are known for being experts in their specialties.

And they are always working.

Gaining a reputation as a specialist will take some time, but once people think of you in a particular way, your track record will become your best sales tool.

But don't get pigeonholed and find that you are

creatively repeating yourself. Before you get straight-jacketed in a trap of your own success, work on mastering a second skill. Then keep expanding your areas of expertise throughout your career.

Versatility will combat your becoming typecast.

RULE

45

Increase your reach, increase your worth.

THE KEY TO advancing in your career is to develop your people skills. If you do your job, then you are worth to your employer only the value of the work that you can personally create. But if you can direct a group of people, then you are worth a great deal more.

Big animated feature films employ hundreds of artists. The talents that command the highest prices are the superstars who can bring the best work out of others. Glen Keane is one of the world's best animators, but where he really stands out is in coaching other artists. His work with the animation department on Disney's *Tangled* improved not only that movie, but also paid dividends on the future films *Wreck-It Ralph* and *Frozen*.

Phil Lord and Christopher Miller are exceptional writers, but their directorial talents really set

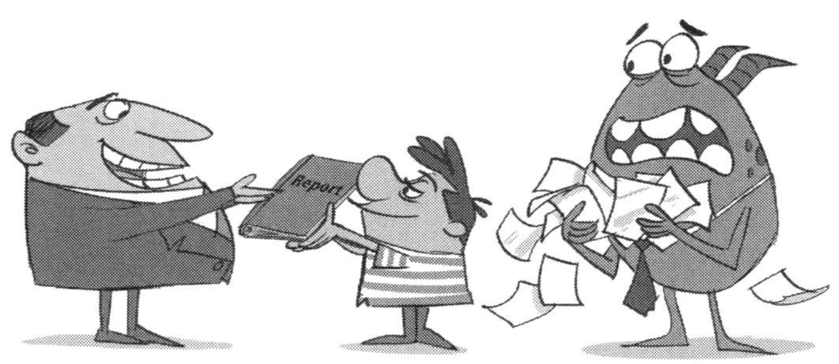

them apart. They have created hit animated features at two different studios: Sony (*Cloudy with a Chance of Meatballs*) and Warner Brothers (*The Lego Movie*)—an almost unprecedented feat. It takes talented direction to convert a screenplay into a great film, and Lord and Miller have done it in both animation and live action.

When you can raise the bar not only for yourself, but also for the others you work with, your value increases exponentially.

RULE

46

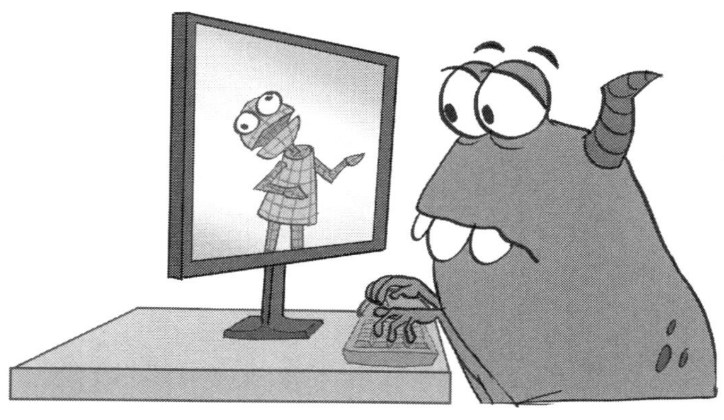

Keep up with what's happening in the industry.

IN 2000, DISNEY closed its traditional, hand-drawn animation department. A few years later, John Lasseter, the Disney creative head, tried to revive the classic craft with *The Princess and the Frog* and a Winnie the Pooh feature, but neither of the films captured the audience as they had hoped. Today, aside from an occasional independent movie, the Hollywood animated feature market is comprised of computer-animated movies.

The transition from hand-drawn animated films to computer-animated films took place over a number of years, but, even so, some artists were surprised when their livelihoods vanished.

Don't allow this to happen to you.

Keep abreast of the trends in your field. The entertainment business is ever changing, and the tools we use today can be obsolete tomorrow. *Variety* was once the must-read periodical of the day, but now that venerable trade magazine has become less relevant than many of its faster-moving digital counterparts.

Protect your career in three ways:

1 Read the trades and stay ahead of trends.
2 Keep up with what other artists, studios, and agencies are doing. Know what is popular.
3 Anticipate what the next tools will be. Pick up the skills of the future right now.

To stay employed, you must stay plugged in.

RULE

47

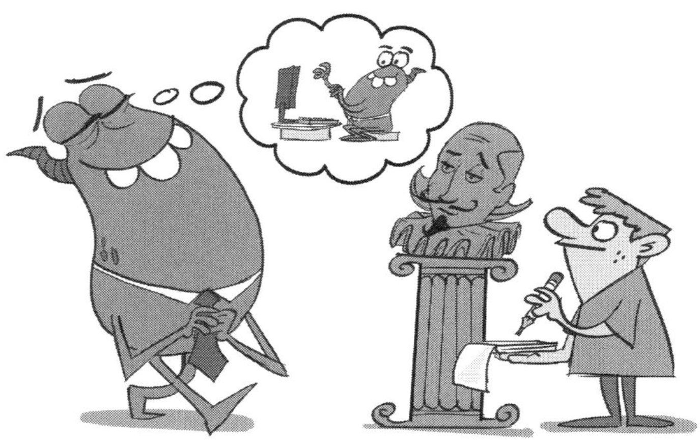

Watch for tastemakers and new platforms.

RECOGNIZE THOSE ARTISTS among your peers who seem to be the next visionaries. Get on their teams.

If you are in a college with a strong animation or film program, watch for classmates who are blossoming. When I moved to Los Angeles in 1979, everyone who had graduated from Cal Arts knew that John Lasseter and Tim Burton were tremendous talents. When I was at New York University, I could see that Chris Columbus and Joel Coen were exceptional. It was apparent early on that Rebecca Sugar (*Steven Universe*) and Phil Lord and Christopher Miller (*The Lego Movie*) would emerge as major players in the animation field. Keep a lookout for people who create exciting work—and try to work with them.

Look for projects that seem to be cutting edge; those can define your career. Some of the artists who were lucky enough to join *The Simpsons* in 1989 ended up with jobs for life. The *South Park* crew has done extremely well, too.

Being associated with a hit project or studio is a surefire way to boost your career. Chris Meledandri was the architect behind Fox's successful launch of Blue Sky Animation with the *Ice Age* movies, and showed his clear talent with *Despicable Me.* While *Surf's Up* and *Iron Giant* were not the successes that Sony and Warner Brothers had hoped for, it was obvious that the film's creators, Chris Buck and Brad Bird, were exceptional. The chance that their next projects, *Frozen* and *The Incredibles* would be hits was improved because of their track record for quality. *Frozen* was also aided by Jennifer Lee—a terrific writer who was crucial to the movie *Wreck-It Ralph.*

It is also wise to follow the new media platforms. The rise of Amazon, Netflix, Google, and YouTube as content providers has created new arenas for artists. The opportunities for short-form entertainment accessible from smartphones may one day outpace traditional television. There may emerge a Walt Disney of the new age.

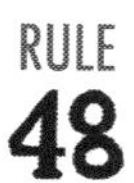

RULE 48

Cerulean is not blue.

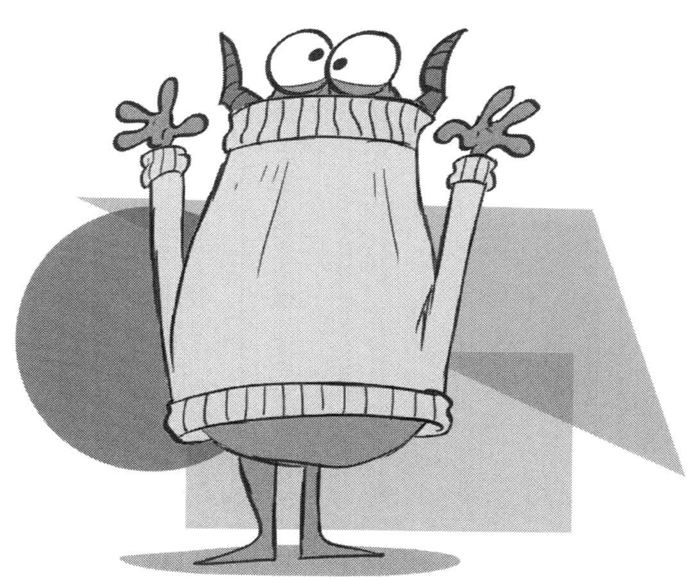

FOREIGN FILMS ARE wonderful. I try to see them whenever I can. I was recounting to a high-ranking studio person why I loved an incredible film from Singapore that I had seen the previous weekend. After I detailed the movie's strengths, the executive shrugged and replied, "Yeah, but no one else is ever going to see it."

The dismissal of that brilliant film set me off.

I ranted: "Did you ever see *The Devil Wears Prada*? There is a scene in the movie where Anne Hathaway, playing a naïve intern, rolls her eyes when she finds her boss, a fashion magazine editor, choosing between two similar-looking green belts. To the intern, the difference between the belts is trivial—no one will notice. But the Anna Wintour-like boss (played by Meryl Streep) rebuts the intern's dismissal with a tour de force tirade by detailing the history of the blue sweater that the Hathaway character is wearing.

"The fashion editor explains that the intern's sweater is not blue, but cerulean. And the color cerulean that she is wearing originated from one visionary fashion designer, who influenced another designer, who, in turn, influenced the clothing lines of stores of different price points, until it finally ended up in the bargain bin that the intern purchased it from."

I added, "The same is true with movies. That's why it is important to see that film from Singapore."

The latest superhero movie may be fun to watch, but that is not where the serious filmmaker is going to gain his or her greatest inspiration. To see the future, you must see the films of the visionaries—Kubrick, Welles, Chris Nolan, Scorsese, Spielberg, and P. T. Anderson, to name just a few.

If all you see are blue sweaters, then you can only make blue sweaters. If you want to be influential, look for cerulean.

RULE

49

Maintain contacts.

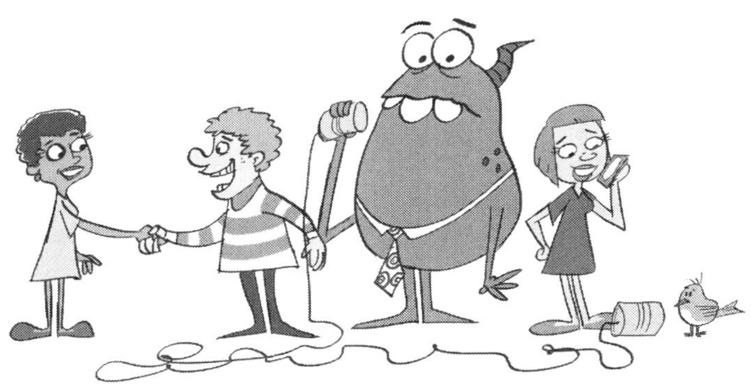

FEATURE ANIMATION ASSIGNMENTS tend to be lengthy, but the artists who work in television animation experience shorter periods of employment. Consequently, artists who create our favorite TV shows become adept at networking.

Working briefly on the television show, *Father of the Pride*, I met a networking genius—the Nijinsky of working the phone.

On a daily basis, I would watch with astonishment as he drew his storyboards while he kept in contact with his friends at the other studios, always gathering information for upcoming jobs. At one moment, he would be speaking with a colleague in Spanish, then call another contact and switch to Filipino. With yet a third contact, he would search for future leads in English.

He knew people at every studio in town, and was conversant on current and future productions. Since so many of his assignments lasted only a few weeks, he needed to be lining up his next job if he wanted to keep employed. Despite his proficiency with networking, he was careful to never overlap his jobs, or compromise his effort at his current job. The longer I sat in the room with him, the more self-conscious I became of my pathetic web of contacts.

Make a deliberate effort to stay in touch with people, and try to know what is going on around town. Don't wait until you are out of work to contact people. If you maintain a network of colleagues while you are employed, you'll have a head start on finding your next job.

RULE
50

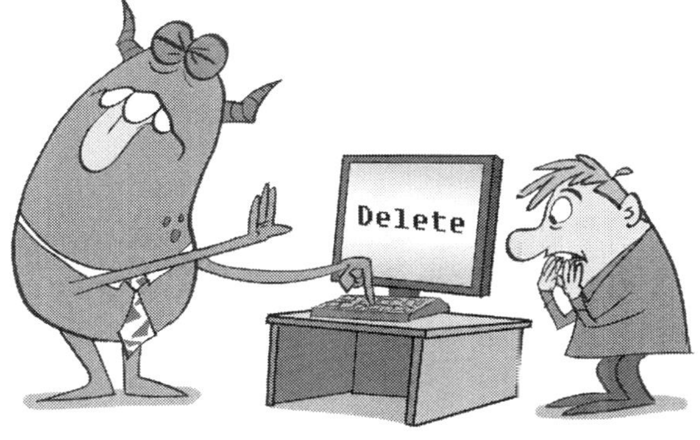

Compliment before critiquing.

OF ALL THE animation rules in this book, this may be the easiest to violate. I have broken it countless times, and I always regret it afterwards. The rule is simple: After an artist has presented you with his/her work, stop for a moment, acknowledge the effort, and find something to compliment. Only then do you offer your critique.

I appreciate it when the person in charge first finds the good in what I have done before suggesting improvements. The process of creating requires that artists deeply invest in their work, and when they present it, artists reveal part of themselves. If you are the person reviewing the work, remember that. Avoid the natural tendency to immediately jump in with your proposed adjustments before first complimenting something.

RULE
51

Don't shoot "good budget."

IN MY EARLY days as a producer, I subscribed to the belief that the movie's budget was a tyrant that I was hired to serve. I would live and die on a weekly basis depending on whether each department was meeting its goals. On a Friday when we had hit our targets, I was relieved. On a week when we fell short, I was filled with anxiety.

Knowing that I was a rookie producer, Amblin surrounded me with two of the best producers in the business: Frank Marshall (*Raiders of the Lost Ark, Poltergeist, The Bourne Identity*) and Robert Watts (the original *Star Wars* trilogy). One day, while I was updating Watts on how the film was falling behind schedule, he must have sensed my increased stress level because he stopped me and asked, "Is the film good?"

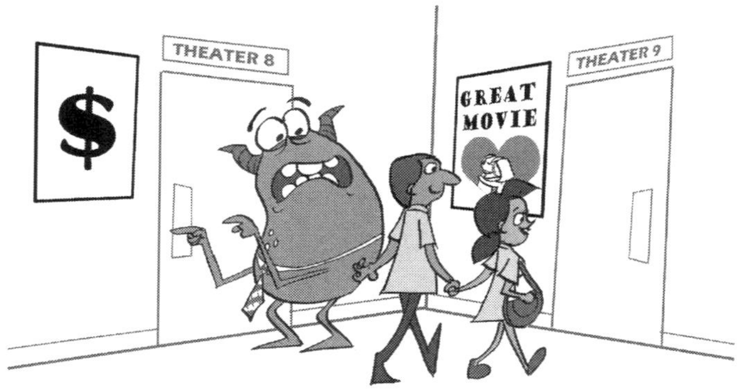

I was so fixated on our budget overages that his question caught me off guard. I recovered and replied, "Yes. Steven (Spielberg) is happy with how it's coming out." Watts then smiled and patted me on the shoulder. "Don't worry. If it's good, we'll get the extra money."

And then he added the words that I had never expected: "Don't be known as someone who shoots 'good budget.'"

Despite the horror stories of Hollywood Studios being known as budget-cutting monsters, that has never been my experience. Robert Watts was right; making a good movie is in everyone's best interests—the filmmakers and the studio. The studio can't make money with a film that stinks even if it does hold to its budget. That was what Watts meant by "shooting 'good budget.'" I learned a vital lesson. Quality is always first.

No studio ever marketed a movie with the tagline: "Came in under budget."

RULE

52

Beat the estimates.

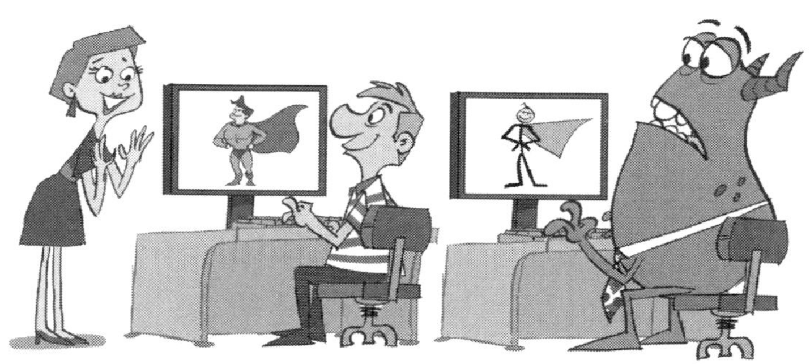

EVERY WEEK, A choreographed dance takes place in the movie business as the entertainment analysts project estimates for the weekend box office, and the studios counter those projections by "managing people's expectations." The result of this numbers game is important to the studios because on the evening of the movie's first day of release, estimates are announced for the weekend box office. If the movie beats the managed expectations, the film is an over-performer—a hit. However, if the movie falls short of those projections, it will be branded with the stigma of being an under-performer—or worse, a flop.

Just like those weekend projections, your career's success also depends on how you measure up to your expectations.

Steve Mason, host of the *Mason and Ireland* show on ESPN radio, said his work philosophy was to "under promise and over deliver."

Create a timetable of delivery that you know you can meet, and then exceed everyone's expectations. If you live this motto, you will stand out.

And now, to beat the estimates,
I offer these three bonus rules . . .

RULE

53

Perform so your work outlasts you.

AS IF THE production of *Who Framed Roger Rabbit?* was not challenging enough, Bob Zemeckis decided to push himself further with his next projects: directing the two *Back to the Future* sequels consecutively.

The schedule turned out to be so grueling on his cast and crew that Zemeckis taped a sign to Michael J. Fox's trailer to light-heartedly remind him of the end game; "Pain is temporary, film is forever." Zemeckis was right. The long shooting hours are now only a memory, but Michael J. Fox will forever be known for his portrayal of Marty McFly.

When I worked at Disney, I knew that every drawing that I created for a film would one day find its way to the Animation Research Library (the morgue). There, my work would rest in the same

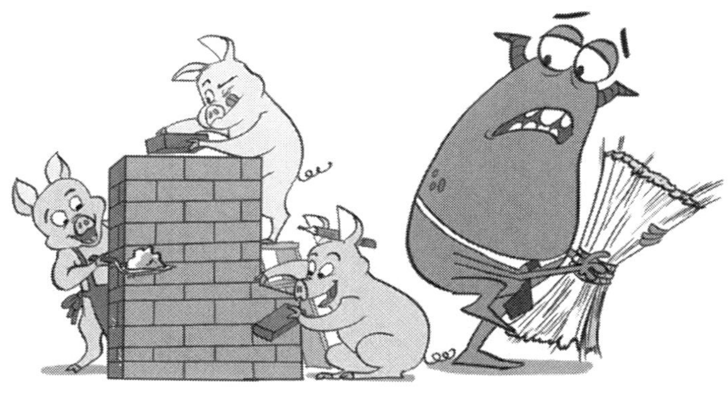

stacks alongside the great artists who created *Snow White and the Seven Dwarfs*, *Pinocchio*, and *Fantasia*. I knew that I could only live in their shadows, but I was proud to be a part of that august history.

Treat every job as part of your legacy.

RULE

54

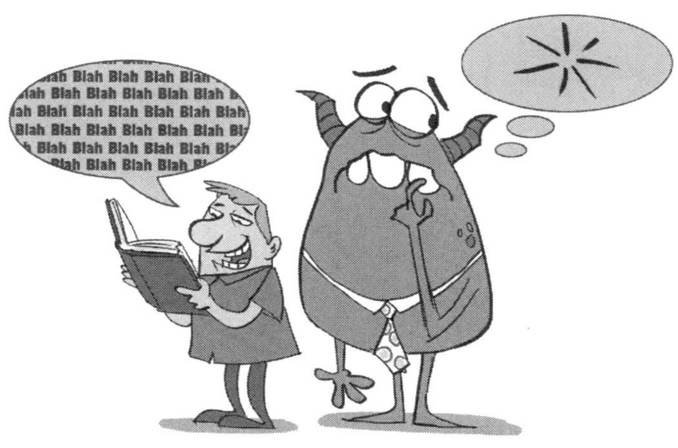

Don't be caught out twice.

AT DAILIES ONE afternoon, the long-time animator Kristof Serrand challenged me to guess which classic film he had used as reference for his animation. I made several guesses, all of which were wrong.

Finally, he revealed his inspiration—Charlie Chaplin's *The Great Dictator*. I love classic movies, but I had never seen that film. But I knew one thing: the next time somebody referenced *The Great Dictator*, I would have seen it.

If someone mentions an artist, movie, or piece of potential research that is relevant to your job assignment and you don't know it, write it down.

Then, look it up later.

Don't be caught out twice on the same material. Ever.

RULE

55

Earn this.

IN *SAVING PRIVATE Ryan*, Tom Hanks plays Captain Miller, who is assigned to find a soldier, Jim Ryan, whose three brothers have been killed in combat. Captain Miller and his division locate Private Ryan, but in the process, Miller is fatally wounded. In Miller's last breaths, he tells the young private to "earn this"—to live a life that is worthy of the cost it took to ensure his safety.

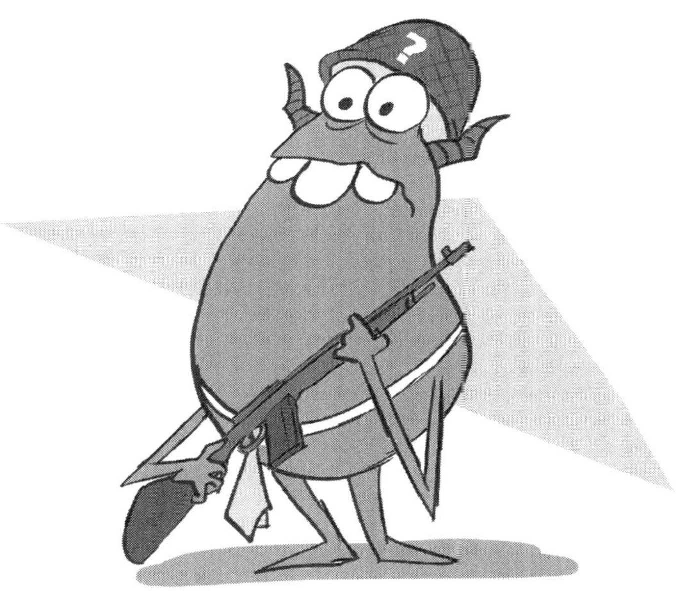

It's a privilege to work in a field as wonderful and fulfilling as entertainment. And this privilege is one we must earn on a daily basis. There are thousands of people who love movies and would like nothing better than to have the opportunity to come to a movie studio to work each day. Earn the right to come to work each day and, if you are lucky enough and persevere, you will have an incredible career.

YOU GOTTA KNOW THE

Rules!

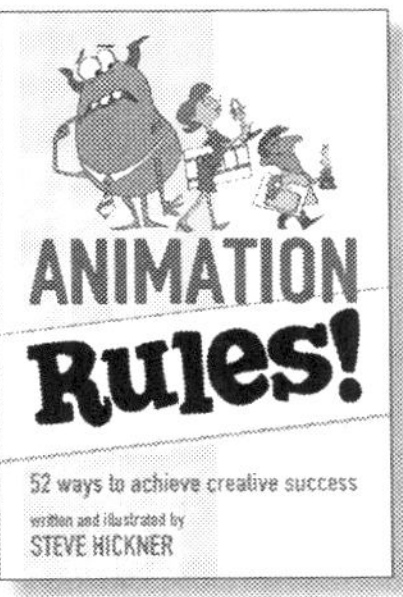

Animation Rules!
by Steve Hickner

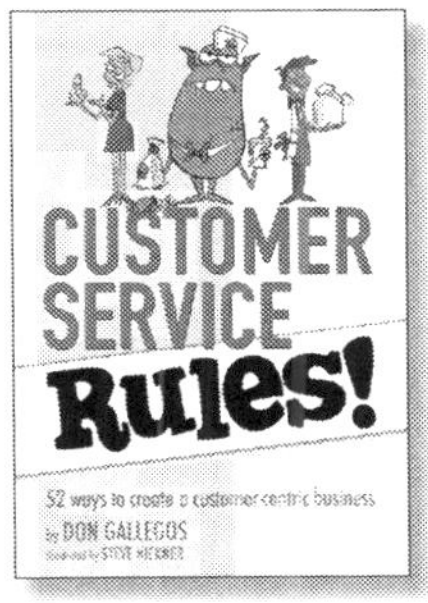

Customer Service Rules!
by Don Gallegos

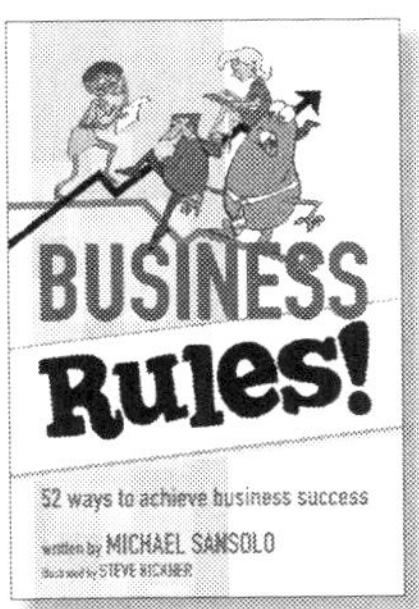

Business Rules!
by Michael Sansolo

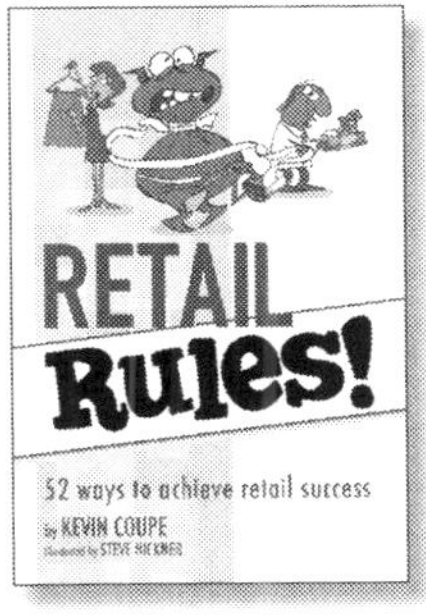

Retail Rules!
by Kevin Coupe

AVAILABLE 2015

Supermarket Rules!
Feedback Rules!
Marketing Rules!
Customer Experience Rules!

To browse our entire collection of **Rules!** books, visit
www.therulesbooks.com

Also by Steve Hickner

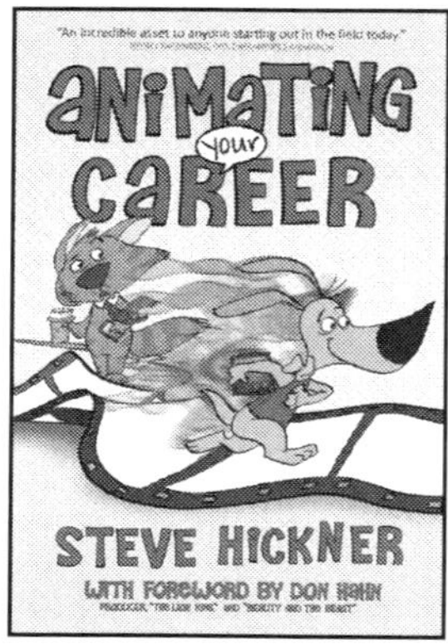

$19.95
ISBN: 978-1-9384062-8-7
190 pp.

Animating Your Career is a valuable guide to navigating the journey of a career in the creative fields—from getting your foot in the door to directing a project involving hundreds of artistic professionals. The book is filled with practical advice from Steve Hickner and the many top creatives he has worked with over the years.

Whether you are still in school and awaiting your first job or are a seasoned professional, Animating Your Career will help guide you to success.

Available at
www.animatingyourcareer.com

Made in the USA
Charleston, SC
12 September 2014